GET RICH

-from the-

P.I.T.C.H.™

NIC MURDOCH

BEng (Elec), JD (HONS 1), MIP, FIPTA, GAICD

Published by mDoch Pty Ltd. *admin@getrichfromthepitch.com*

Cover Design, Editing & Distribution: Entourage Media *entouragemedia.ca*

Back Cover Photography & Author Bio Photograph: Glenn Hunt

To request permissions, contact the publisher at
admin@getrichfromthepitch.com

ISBN (Paperback Edition): 978-0-9756557-0-2
ISBN (eBook Edition): 978-0-9756557-1-9

First Paperback Edition: March 2024

Printed in Australia

To all the inventors out there: thank you.
The world would be a boring place without you.

To my children: plot twist; you are both adopted.

To Vern: thanks for putting up with me.

To my parents, Ann and Arthur: I told you I'd finish the book.
[PS - Thank you. PPS - Miss you Mum.]

CONTENTS

I'M NOT YOUR LAWYER

We're living in a gig economy where one idea can spark revolutions, reshape your destiny, and change the trajectory of the world. Just as we covet gold, perhaps we should be coveting ideas. After all, they can be *far* more valuable.

Since you picked up this book, I have a few questions for you:

- How many notebooks do you have lying around your home or office, filled with ideas that came to you in moments of inspiration or clarity?
- How many times have you experienced the entrepreneurial rush of adrenaline that happens when a brilliant idea strikes?
- How many times have you grabbed a sticky note and pen to sketch out potential sales numbers for one of those ideas, detailing how many widgets you'd have to sell to make $100, $100,000, $100,000,000?

- How many times have you thought to yourself, "That could be a game-changer…"

And then the most important question of all:

- How many times was that the place where your idea died, destined to never make it off the page, soon to be done by someone else instead?

When you keep your ideas to yourself, they happily live on, rent-free in your head, not changing the world, and certainly not filling your pockets with riches.

As an inventor, you have a remarkable gift, a true talent, and others will want *in*, whether that means joining your team, funding your dream, or sadly, doing their best to steal your idea.

Inventors often fail to get an idea off the ground, not because the idea lacks merit—far from it. Inventors fail because they don't know how to:

- start,
- validate their idea,
- avoid or overcome inventor syndrome,
- scale,
- choose the right people for their start-up squad,
- find a co-founder with the same vision,
- find investors for the various rounds of funding (who to ask for what and when),

- pitch the idea to the people who can help make it happen,
- protect their idea before it's worth a fortune.

We live in a world where opportunists, those who don't have your talent, will take advantage of you. Your inventiveness isn't just a talent; it's a beacon for admirers and opportunists. That means that to be successful in bringing your invention to market, you will need to protect yourself and your talent.

I'm Nic Murdoch. I'm a seasoned technology lawyer who's been creating and inventing for over twenty-five years. I help people just like you protect their ideas, paving the way to generational prosperity. I've also watched as unprotected ideas are 'stolen' by opportunists from underneath well-meaning but overly zealous inventors who went to market too early, looking for a quick payday and, as a result, exposed to risk.

Every day, technology lawyers just like me witness remarkable inventors and founders grappling with the challenge of piercing their marketplace with inventions because they do not know how the innovation industry works, they don't know what makes a start-up successful, or because others outright steal the idea out from under them. Worse still, these otherwise intelligent entrepreneurs are unaware it's their own actions that often lead to their inevitable failure.

The purpose of this book is to motivate you to take the leap into invention, show you how to capitalize off of your brilliant ideas, aid you as an inventor or entrepreneur, to protect yourself before you launch your trillion-dollar idea, and to teach you how to capitalize on your personality type, your skill set, and your killer idea for a successful launch into the marketplace. I will guide you to move from inventor to successful exit—whatever that exit looks like for you.

My passion lies in protecting the talent of inventors just like you. I've seen the good, the bad, and the ugly of the innovation industry, and I'm here to teach you about what I have learned.

I've advised clients who turn over billions. I've guided mergers and acquisitions of intellectual property (IP) valued at over a billion dollars, and I've litigated intellectual property matters where the potential damages run into hundreds of millions. Numbers only scratch the surface. More important to you is that I have an uncanny ability to guide inventors to protect their ideas and steer start-ups to achieve sustainable growth, innovate industries, and create generational wealth.

I'm elated that my life and expertise have brought me to this point—to uniquely understand, protect, and champion innovations, inventions, and, most importantly, inventors.

If you are thinking big and want to go from big idea to big payday, listen up: inside the pages of this book are insights, strategies, and insider secrets designed to help you turn your ideas into fortune.

If you've been looking not only to enter but to dominate in the marketplace, this book is for you.

* * *

To understand how I got here, I want you to picture the 1980s in Townsville, North Queensland, Australia. It's a coastal town right next to the amazing Great Barrier Reef and in the shadow of Magnetic Island, which, at that time, was home to WikiLeaks founder Julian Assange.

The 80s weren't all wild haircuts and neon outfits (but weren't they wonderful?). Television was limited to ABC and Channel 7—so beyond the news, *The Curiosity Show*, and *Doctor Who*, you pretty much entertained yourself. The internet was non-existent, and children, including me, found ourselves playing outdoors, where we'd stay until the sun set—our sign it was home time. It was the best of times and a wonderful time to be alive.

Back then, I was a bit of (okay, a lot of) a tomboy.

I spent all my free time in my father's backyard shed, handing him his wrench or oil can as he lovingly restored (with my help!) a vintage Model T Ford. In truth, I was less of a "build it, and they will come" and more of a break it and rebuild it better kind of child. Still, the dissection of toys and Model Ts awoke an insane thirst for understanding how everything around me worked … especially if it could be ripped apart and reassembled.

I have always been a tinkerer, an inventor, and a creator. Or, as my mother once deemed me, "a menace to every toy" I ever saw. These seemingly mundane childhood explorations would set the stage for my rare convergence of skills as an engineer, my training as a patent agent and, later, career as a technology lawyer.

My love of tearing things apart to explore left me with a pretty unique skill set. Following my love of "build, tear apart, rinse, and repeat," I graduated with an electrical engineering degree and worked in computer programming. I took everything I learned and applied it to unravel the complex and make it simple. Intricate designs, mechanics, and algorithms truly felt like works of art to me.

But, I grew tired of engineering (or re-engineering) things. So, I turned my attention to the law, graduating *summa cum laude* with a Juris Doctor (a law degree for post-grads). In that transition, I discovered a passion for intellectual property and an age-old tradition intricately woven into the fabric of safeguarding and asserting ownership over inventions—a practice known as patenting. This process fascinated me and demonstrated the intersection between technology and the law of protecting valuable information and ideas. I earned a master's degree on the topic and trained to be a patent agent (or patent attorney as it's known in my area of the world) so I could draft patents for inventors to help them protect ideas. At the same time, I qualified as a trademark attorney to safeguard brand identities.

What truly made me a leader in the intellectual property field was, well, *all of it*.

My background in engineering and my knowledge of law showed me the value of ideas and how they can be transformed into something salable. It also taught me that not everyone is an inventor, and those who can't invent often steal.

These days, I am the managing director of EAGLEGATE, a law firm in Brisbane, Australia. We specialize in commercial law, litigation, intellectual property, and technology law to protect intellectual property, guide clients in corporate legal issues, and litigate when rights are infringed or to defend our client's right to trade. I have handled thousands of intellectual property infringement matters, and I still gain a certain satisfaction from holding an idea thief accountable or defending a client against a bully who oversteps their boundaries.

To keep life interesting, I occasionally jump in as a non-executive director or in an advisory role to help companies get off the ground, break into new markets, navigate technology changes, keep their IP on lockdown, and sort out their cyber and information security issues.

My background is the best of both worlds: technical know-how and legal dexterity. Most importantly for you, my experiences have taught me that there are two types of inventors. There are the insiders—those who invent in their own industry and are already in business, with their sales game on point and a ready market eager to purchase their newest invention. And then there are the outsiders—those who invent outside their industry and may not have a track record in business or the innovation industry. These folks usually struggle with how to get their product out there. Even if they've done their research, flying solo will be risky if they don't have the right mix of skills, the personality for the industry, or the marketing and financial resources to really make a splash.

This book is the sum of my experience in IP, laid

out in black and white for you. I'm applying over 25 years of experience to the following pages.

Get Rich from the P.I.T.C.H.™ isn't merely another business book. It's an almanac of wisdom, offering profound insights from someone deeply immersed in the world of intellectual property and its fortification. As you learn and follow the P.I.T.C.H. Method™, you're effectively being given a masterclass on safeguarding, cultivating, and masterfully showcasing your innovative ideas to achieve your end goal (and we'll discuss your end-goal options later).

This book underscores the value of even the simplest of ideas. So, if you've picked up these pages thinking you need a groundbreaking patentable idea—think again!

Perhaps you've:

- spotted a gap in the market for an existing retailer, want to pitch your idea, and sit back and enjoy the royalties. You'll learn how to pitch your idea effectively and safely while securing a slice of the pie for yourself;
- invented the next fidget spinner and want to spin your way into mega money from kids pestering their parents to buy a fun and irresistibly cheap toy. We'll teach you how to protect that

idea worldwide and perhaps even sell it to the highest bidder;

- overcome a long-held problem every new parent faces and want to share your insights, but want to protect yourself at the same time. We'll teach you your best options to make money out of the idea (hint: it isn't what you think), how to find the perfect investor for you, how to pitch to investors, what investors think, and what they are looking for in the idea and in you; or

- invented a widget so inventive it's a paradigm shift. You'll learn what personalities your start-up squad needs to take the idea to market or whether you are more suited to a different, but still lucrative, end goal.

What is the P.I.T.C.H. Method?

If you're ready to get rich, you're going to want to start here.

P.I.T.C.H. is a simple methodology to take you from validating your idea to protecting the idea, to determining whether you have what it takes to be a sole founder or whether you need a start-up squad, to setting your end goal in place and pitching to investors.

It will elevate you from simply being an inventor to being a trailblazer.

It is a process for ensuring your t's are crossed, and i's are dotted every step of the way so that you and the idea are safe, secure, and successful.

Inside this book, you'll learn every element of The P.I.T.C.H. Method:

> **Prepare to Validate:** You must test the waters of reality and determine if your idea is a sinker or a swimmer. This is your litmus test of determining if the market is ready for your genius.
>
> **IP IQ:** Learn how, where, and when to protect your ideas from those who want to claim your ideas as their own.
>
> **Test Your Type:** Personality type plays a big part in the success or failure of an idea making it to market. Are you cut out to be a sole founder, or do you need a start-up squad? Discover the personality traits of successful start-ups and your strengths and weaknesses.
>
> **Chart Your Exit:** Learn the different end goals for inventors and decide what path to wealth you wish to take. Hint: you don't need to launch a start-up to make money from ideas. You could cash in as early as tomorrow.

Harness Your Capital: Learn about investors, what they are looking for, investment and funding cycles, and how to pitch based on your stage of commercialization to achieve your chosen end goal.

The P.I.T.C.H. Method is a framework that will guide you through a well-trodden path formerly walked by every successful inventor—even if they don't know it at the time.

Inside these coveted pages, you'll find stories from the field—the real stuff you won't find in the news, and some you will.

It's important to know that no confidences are ever breached in sharing these stories. Each of the stories, smart business practices, illegal business practices, strategies, and scams set out in this book are not rare. In fact, they affect millions around the world. The stories and lessons learned repeat themselves in different industries for different inventors time and again. Sometimes the lessons shared in the stories are retained with the names, inventions, scenarios, and industries changed and modified to protect those in the innovation industry—the good, the bad, and the stupid. Importantly, whilst I spill the beans on the innovation industry and share industry insider secrets, I am not letting you in on any client secrets.

These are the lessons of what works, what doesn't,

how to keep your ideas yours, and how you can strategize your way to P.I.T.C.H. success for yourself.

Whether your idea is big or small, this book will guide you through protecting it and priming it for success, and your first step is to perfect the art of the P.I.T.C.H.

Not everyone wants to pitch an idea, but if you have an idea or invention, you will have to at some point—whether it's to a potential start-up team member, an investor, or your target buyer. A pitch does not need to be a long, drawn-out death by PowerPoint. It just has to be good. A pitch is simply a sales pitch. It can be as short or as long as you (and your audience) can tolerate. In the following chapters, I use the word pitch to mean sell—how to sell your big idea and what you need to educate your audience to have them eating out of the palm of your hand. In the final chapter, I teach you how to create a Pitch Deck.

Perhaps you are lucky enough to bootstrap your idea (meaning using your own funds), but at some point in the future, you will need to pitch. Whether that is to sell your invention (and run with the money), launch into a different marketplace, expand your product range, or take your company to the stock exchange, **you will need to pitch**.

Now, a word of caution, dear P.I.T.C.H.er, this

won't be pretty. Innovation, invention, and IP protection can be a messy business, making lots of dirty laundry. It's more like an episode of *Game of Thrones* than *Bluey*. This book will show you the triumphs but also the fierce, vindictive battles, cunning maneuvers, and shocking betrayals in the world of idea protection and commercialization and the journey you're embarking upon.

While other books tiptoe around the darker corners of IP litigation, here, we embrace them, offering you a front-row seat to the gritty confrontations that arise when ideas, often worth billions, are at stake. From backstabbing collaborators and corporate espionage to high-stakes courtroom dramas, this book promises a raw, unfiltered exploration of the lengths individuals and corporations will go to claim, protect, or steal a groundbreaking idea.

This journey promises not just enlightenment but also a taste of the bitter battles that sometimes define the world of intellectual property. There lies an unspoken rule within legal circles, particularly in intellectual property protection, echoing the sentiments of the famed *Fight Club* in that we don't talk about the battles. Yet, much like the famed Brad Pitt movie, the fights over intellectual property can be intense, relentless, and game-changing—and often not talked about. Here, we break that silence, pulling back the curtain because it has come time to talk about the boxing ring.

And court action (litigation) is a boxing ring because you don't know when the next round of blows will come. Throughout this book, I don't want to make light of your inventions or the complex challenges inventors face when trying to launch their ideas into the world. However, I do use analogies to turn complex concepts into clear pictures for us all. You may find them silly or funny or entertaining … good! I want that. The last thing the world needs is another unused, boring business book written by a lawyer. So, we look at and laugh at ourselves along the way. The best way we learn is through storytelling, and inside these pages, I do a lot of that.

I take a lighthearted look at the boxing ring battles, but make no mistake: the boxing ring is serious, and sometimes it's a fight for survival. Don't mistake my light-hearted references for a lack of concern; I am fully cognizant of the physical, emotional, and financial damage of the boxing ring. In the area of intellectual property, fights come with the territory. You need to know what you are walking into, the boxing ring included.

While I'm sharing my knowledge and experience, it's essential to remember that this is not legal advice.

For that, you'll have to seek your very own counsel who has experience in this area of law. I'm *a* lawyer, but I'm not *your* lawyer.

And even though these stories may mirror what you have been through or what you are going through, that does not mean they are about you; in this field, the details may change but the stories repeat over and over.

This book contains general information on the innovation industry and cannot speak to your specific circumstances. Before relying on anything in this book, you need to seek qualified legal counsel in the appropriate country. Intellectual property protection laws vary wildly around the world. What works in one country may not work in another; in fact, the laws are often polar opposites. Search engines are sure to give you advice written by people who are either in the wrong country for your situation, or who are simply wrong. AI is about the same ... so far.

This book should, ideally, be read cover-to-cover by inventors, entrepreneurs, founders, financiers, and marketers who want to know more about IP and making money from ideas. To all the aspiring P.I.T.C.H.ers of the future, I encourage you to devour its contents, grab your highlighter, and extract any lessons that resonate with your journey.

Brace yourself for an adventure through the pages

of knowledge and possibility! Before you embark on this journey, here's a cheeky heads-up: the techniques and strategies nestled within these pages are much like a box of assorted chocolates—you never know what you're gonna get.

I've put together a smorgasbord of ideas that could potentially catapult you to stardom, or … well, not. It's like flipping a coin with the universe—sometimes you land heads, sometimes tails, and sometimes the coin rolls under the couch, never to be seen again.

I can't promise you'll be the next big thing since sliced bread. What I can offer is a journey of discovery, a few laughs, and perhaps even an "Aha!" moment or two.

As you delve deeper into the following chapters, you'll discover the true value it holds for your endeavors. Your success may just depend on it. So dive into the pages of this book and discover the most profound advice I've ever encountered, etched on the side of a wooden study desk: "Your task is simple: reduce the distance between what you know and what you should."

Let this book be your guide in closing the divide between your current knowledge and the wisdom you need to fulfill your dreams.

Let your journey of getting rich from your P.I.T.C.H. begin.

CHAPTER TWO

DOES THIS HAVE LEGS?

(a.k.a. Prepare to Validate)

First of all, congratulations on creating a unique idea that has the possibility of making an impact on the world—or at the very least, your finances. It takes a special mind to do this. Not everyone was born an innovator, creator, or inventor. It's a feat all on its own. Enjoy this moment.

In this chapter, we will discover whether your idea is a money-maker or not. Not every big idea comes with a big payout.

The Birth of Ideas

Many people believe invention starts with a brilliant idea or spark of inspiration. But that comes after you identify a problem that needs to be solved. People who have had a spark of inspiration have already identified the problem to be solved, sometimes without realizing it. In IP circles, identifying the problem to be solved is often referred to as identifying the problem scope. For example, you may be tired of having to carry your identification cards. Here, the problem scope is clear: how can individuals be identified without relying on traditional ID cards?

The second step is to consider how to overcome the problem. Perhaps you could use a person's fingerprint, eye scan, pass number, or face print for identification purposes? So here we have an idea for a solution to the problem, but we don't yet know if it is even feasible.

The third step is where the magic of the "inventive step" (a legal term in patenting) and "inventive genius" comes into play. That is, the inventor has an inventive spark or a unique and novel way to bring the possible solution to life to solve the problem. It's *that* particular solution that becomes the marketable product that generates the flow of money.

I lied to you. And I am not sorry.

In the introduction, I spoke about protecting ideas but doing so isn't possible in reality. You can't protect ideas alone. Rather, it's the solution that can be protected from others. In IP circles, the invention is the *solution*, rather than the invention being a *mere idea*. This is how intellectual property laws operate, including what they protect and the need to disclose how the solution is built, which we will delve into later.

If the inventor solves a problem in a manner that none have done before (in patenting terms, that means it is novel), they *may* have an invention that can be protected through that very old system I discussed earlier—patenting.

Protecting solutions is your best approach because the money you're looking for doesn't flow from mere ideas. Instead, your earnings and profit come from bringing that idea to life by creating a solution that overcomes the problem. That is where the real treasure lies.

And that follows the innovation industry: winning ideas and successful founders are most often motivated by impact, not money or fame.

The more people who want to find a solution to the problem they are facing (i.e., the size of the marketplace), the more the idea (or rather, the solution) is successful. In simple terms, a winning idea represents an opportunity in *that* marketplace at *that* time, but a losing idea does not.

For example, space tourism is currently extraordinarily expensive because it is tasked with offsetting the cost of development since everyone is new to the market. Vacationing with aliens doesn't (yet!) have a strong market appeal, but with climate change and world calamities on the rise, perhaps it's time just has not come *yet*! Eventually, the cost of space tourism will come down. The idea is a good one, but it isn't going to make anybody rich quickly. It's going to take further development and research before the space tourism pitch makes anyone mega-rich (but, I'll admit, I can see it coming)!

The truth is everyone has ideas, but very few of them are worthy of being brought to life or are innovative inventions (i.e., money-making worthy).

Your task, when reading this chapter, is to determine whether your idea is a chart-topper or just a flash in the pan—it's time to separate the blockbusters from the busts. Let's find out if your invention or idea is your ticket to riches!

Idea v Opportunity

We, collectively, have several hundred ideas throughout the course of our days. They may occur standing in your shower, when you think, "I just wish I had something to write my ideas down in the shower" (yes, this has already been invented), or "Someone should make a way for golf balls to be better for the environment." (Sorry – that one is taken as well.)

Not all ideas or inventions have an opportunity attached to them, and obviously, not every idea or invention is a good one.

CASE STUDY: There is an invention that places an expectant mother onto a device that will then spin her to use centrifugal force to deliver the baby. I wish I were joking, but it's a real patent (we'll learn about patents in the next chapter) with the title of "APPARATUS FOR FACILITATING THE BIRTH OF A CHILD BY CENTRIFUGAL FORCE," the purpose of which is "to provide an apparatus which will assist the under-equipped woman by creating a gentle, evenly distributed, properly directed, precision-controlled force, that acts in unison with and supplements her own efforts."

Follow the link[1] at the footer to see grizzly images of the device. For those concerned that the device will work too well and the baby will be launched like a projectile only to snap back under the elasticity of the umbilical cord, fear not. The invention included a handy net to catch the baby.

Dear P.I.T.C.H.er, you are probably thinking this is an 1800s torture device, but no; it was invented in 1965 by a man <u>and a woman</u>, George and Charlotte Blonsky, who were reportedly a childless New York couple, which may explain why they optimistically

---

1   Blonsky, George B, Charlotte E Blonsky, and Individual. "US3216423A - Apparatus for Facilitating the Birth of a Child by Centrifugal Force - Google Patents," n.d. https://patents.google.com/patent/US3216423A/en.

chose the word "gentle" when describing how the device operated. ∎

To find out if your idea is a profitable opportunity, you'll need to determine if it is needed, if it's the right time for it, and if there's value in it. With no offense to Mr. and Mrs. Blonsky, I can't envision a time when their invention solves a need in the marketplace.

Let's look at a less extreme example. We have an electric car that needs to be charged, but it is parked for a good part of the day. That is fine when we are home, as we can use a granny charger to charge it in our own garage. But what if we travel and can't get to a fast charger? Or, what if we're at work and have nowhere to plug in our granny charger? What if we didn't have a garage? How would we charge it?

Imagine if homeowners opened up their garages for people like me. All they would need is a charging station meter plugged into an electrical point, and I could use my own granny charger.

Now, let's throw in an app that tells me where these granny chargers are, when they are available, and the rate charged by the homeowner. Great, I can definitely see the implementation of the idea, and there is a need in the marketplace. However, the immediate problem I would face is the likelihood of a short window of implementation, given that service stations will soon be installing more and more fast chargers. Therefore, the opportunity is temporal.But is it an opportunity or just an idea?

In my current environment, it isn't an opportunity because there is not much money in it for a homeowner, given the inconvenience of having someone parked in their garage all day. The current cost of charging a car is low, and it takes many hours to fully charge an EV on a granny charger, which is inconvenient for the homeowner. So, the homeowner wouldn't be compensated enough for the inconvenience—for now.

No money = no charge, honey.

But this solution may be an opportunity in other countries as their service stations are compensating for the loss of dinosaur juice sales by ramping up the cost of electric charging. So there is an opportunity in other countries.

The homeowner could charge slightly less than the service stations with the added benefit of letting me park all day and make a sale. It's not price fixing if you are merely being competitive.

If the name didn't already clue you in, granny chargers are chargers for electric vehicles that plug into a normal power point. It's essentially an extension cord straight from a power source. They are aptly named because of their slowness.

This is the difference between an idea and an opportunity. There may be a need for a solution to the problem I am experiencing, but this solution won't work right now in my marketplace, as it is not financially viable. But it might be viable later.

Steps to Invention Validation:

1. **Define your customer base**
2. **Define the market**
3. **Analyze the competition**
4. **Analyze the feasibility**
5. **Define your unique value proposition (UVP)**
6. **Conduct a SWOT analysis**

This may look something like the start of a business plan. That's because it is. The overall purpose of this analysis is to educate whether the idea is a viable opportunity.

To get a good overview of where you stand in the market, what opportunities are available, and where you want to head after all of this analysis, you need to assess:

- Who are your customers? What do your

customers want? What pains are they suffering that you are curing?

- What is the size of the marketplace? What percentage of people are in the market for the solution? What percentage of those people could you reasonably sell to? Can you sell it repeatedly to those people?
- Who are your competitors, and what are they selling? What are their strengths and weaknesses? What is your value proposition, and why should customers buy your product over the competitor's product?
- Can you protect the idea from competitors? Will competitors simply launch the same solution to the problem after you reveal your solution? What would stop them from doing that?
- What are the barriers to entry? What stops people from entering the same marketplace, and are they an obstacle to you? What laws and regulations might apply? What other barriers to the market are there?
- How are you going to have the product manufactured? Where are you distributing the product? What are your distribution channels?
- Is this viable? What are you charging? How are you charging? What is your expected profit?

- What is your SWOT?

All of this information is of interest to investors and what you need to know for your pitch to investors or idea buyers.

Step 1: Define your Customer Base

Get familiar with your audience. The quickest way to do so is to ask four simple questions:

- Who are your customers?
- What do they want?
- What do they need?
- What pain points are they currently experiencing around the problem scope and does your product offer the solution?

In our EV example, there are two customers: the EV owner and the homeowner. One is a person with an EV who either doesn't have a home charger or needs to charge outside of their home—perhaps a person who lives in an apartment that is not permitted to install a charger in their garage, or someone who doesn't have a garage at all. The second customer is a homeowner who wants to make money on the side and has an empty spot on their land where a car can be parked for hours at a time.

I'm sure we could use Google for our market research or just use our imaginations, but we're savvy P.I.T.C.H.ers, which means we're going to go straight to the source—our potential customers.

Successful corporations invest millions (if not billions) in focus groups prior to any major launch. They want to ensure the packaging, messaging, and product fit their ideal customer's needs and wants, as well as solve their problem. You need qualitative insights. Without that, you're left with boxes of unused, unopened merchandise that becomes landfill instead of solution.

You need to get to know your potential customer.

A point on consumer research: an underserved tool is observational research—legal 'stalking' of your audience to see how they interact with your product. This could include handing out your product at expos to see how they interact with, modify, create, or even destroy your product. Fun fact: often, your potential customer might even find new uses for your invention.

Let them play with your product because watching your customer interact with, destroy, and rebuild your product may just identify a need the customer is facing that you never even considered. This may open up your product to new applications and new markets.

Viagra[2] was initially tested as a treatment for angina, but after the testing, certain patients asked for more meds. Don't be afraid to pivot based on customer needs. You may just give your customers a new lease on life.

CASE STUDY: A friend is in the laundry industry and services Airbnb-style accommodation providers. In short, he does their dirty washing and returns it to the Airbnb nicely pressed and clean. He keeps track of the washing and knows exactly how many towels, bed sheets, pillow slips, etc., are provided by each Airbnb. From that, he can do the math to determine each Airbnb's general occupancy rate. Now, that occupancy rate would be confidential to each Airbnb, but whether it is confidential once it is de-identified and mixed with other data is another matter.

He saw an opportunity to service the individual Airbnb but also to use the laundry he is given to generate reports on occupancy in the general area, between different types of Airbnb accommodation and to identify trends over time.

In short, he pivoted once he saw a customer need.

---

2   Wikipedia contributors. "Sildenafil." Wikipedia, February 23, 2024. https://en.wikipedia.org/wiki/Sildenafil.

What made that idea an opportunity was that he sold the reports back to the very Airbnbs that gave him the dirty laundry he relied on to make his reports accurate!

Why does the Airbnb owner pay for the reports? Because the Airbnb business wants to benchmark itself. The owner wants to know if its occupancy is down compared to the competition or whether the industry as a whole is being hit.

Benchmarking yourself against the competition is an important tool to test business health. The twist was that during a downturn in the industry, he was making more money from selling the reports than he was from his laundry services.

He identified his customer base and the problems they were facing, then gave them a solution to their pain points. ∎

The lesson here is don't be afraid to pivot, even after you've been in the market a while.

Think outside the box. Where else can you find customers? Are the customers you want to target your only potential customers?

Think of a vertical line and a horizontal line. On the vertical line are those above and beneath you in the chain of sales—your suppliers and those who buy from you to sell or use the product themselves. Horizontally, is your competition. Can you sell to your competition?

I work with someone who writes software in the business planning industry. He is brilliant at identifying a need in the marketplace for those users, but he is a terrible salesperson. To be honest, he is just lacking when it comes to sales.

He worked out that his competitors loved his platform but had no clue how few customers he had. They assumed he had thousands of customers when he just didn't. He also hated the sales part of his business. He had a choice to make: merge with others or stay the sole founder and pivot. I talk about personality types in later chapters, but he was a perfect example of someone who needed to either work by himself and service only a few customers or work in a team. The problem was he didn't want a team, and he wasn't a person who liked other people—he preferred the company of computers.

He played to his strengths and approached his competitors with an offer to license his software to them where he would take a cut of the fee charged to every customer by the competitor. Importantly, he would no longer need to make the sale to users of the software himself. He would badge the software with the competitor's logo, and the user wouldn't even know they were using his software. But it got better. He didn't want to hand over his software to the competition, so he hosted the software on his servers and charged his competitors hosting fees. Best part? He was happy in the company of his computers—a win/win thanks to licensing—and he got to keep doing what he loved while his competitors got the product and did what they loved. He is so successful now that he no longer sells on the vertical—only the horizontal.

Customers are everywhere; sometimes, you have to find them under rocks, and sometimes they are sitting right beside you.

Step 2: Define the Market

Market analysis, simply put, allows us to identify the potential market size, evaluate any growth opportunities, and see market trends.

Sometimes your analysis will reveal market gaps and even timing components. Now may not be the time to launch, but it doesn't mean the idea is a dud. Follow the analysis. Getting it right at the right time can lead to a market sweep and a big payout later.

Your invention isn't worth inventing if it doesn't serve someone or something. So ask yourself these questions:

- What percentage of people are in the market for the solution?
- What percentage of those people could I reasonably sell to?
- Can I sell it repeatedly to my customers?

Determining your market size allows you to identify the revenue opportunity for your product. You don't want to walk into a pitch with potential investors and say, "Here is my great invention. One person in the world will buy it."

You'd be laughed out of the room.

However, what if you walked in saying there are eight billion people in the world and 25 percent (two billion) of them face this problem? We can reasonably expect to sell to 10 percent of those two billion people, but what if our product has a life span of 100 uses, and it then needs to be replaced? We can resell to those two hundred million people every month, and with a profit margin of $5 per sale, make a profit margin of $1 billion per month. No one is laughing now.

Apply that logic to a fidget spinner. That was a fantastic idea and a fantastic product. It was priced low for each marketplace to ensure that it was a small value purchase—the type of purchase that no one thinks twice about before making. Not only that but it could have been sold multiple times over to every person in the world. A low-value product is easily lost and easily replaced.

To determine your market size, you need to investigate your market through publications, surveys, and the like. Depending on the product, that may be public knowledge. For instance, online real estate companies may produce market research documentation. If you are targeting demographic and economic data, look at local census bureaus or government reports. Google Trends also allows you to determine search trends; this is a handy tool to determine what goods may be increasing in popularity. You can even "see what's trending now." Also, try industry associations and statistical agencies.

You may be able to conduct this research yourself, but if not, there are services that can assist.

Once you know the market size, you can determine the available market (which is the market if you were to achieve 100 percent of sales), the serviceable market (which is the size of the market given your area and other constraints), and your service obtainable market (which is the size of the market you could reasonably service).

It's often far better to underestimate by just a wee bit, rather than to inflate or overinflate your figures.

Let's look at a fun example, shall we? I'm a big fan of *The Big Bang* Theory. There's this great episode where the guys (Sheldon, Raj, Leonard & Howard) are building a math equation app. While messy co-founder situations ensue between Sheldon and the guys, resulting in him being tossed off the project, Penny intervenes with her own app idea for helping people source shoes online.

With the math equation app in the rearview, Sheldon helps Penny create the shoe app. While the episode itself doesn't outright say it, Penny's shoe app idea would likely make Sheldon and her successful far faster than the guys' app would. Why? Mass appeal.

Mass appeal = more money in an initial offer.

Step 3: Analyze the Competition:

One of the greatest assets you'll ever have as an inventor is knowing your competition better than you know yourself.

Let's look at Google versus Apple. Apple saw an ability to sell smartphones into the market. Google, however, figured out how to produce smartphones cheaper and then made the operating system open source—effectively rendering Apple as a higher-priced option for a very similar thing. By analyzing their competition, Google chose to compete on a totally different level.

Analyze what your competition does well and what

it does poorly and question whether you can do it better. Often, over-eager, get-rich-quick inventors will walk away once they realize they have competition. They think "first to market" is the only way to success. It is not. The first to market does not always win.

Google was not the first search engine, Facebook was not the first social media site, and eBay was not the first second-hand goods website. What each of these companies did was analyze the marketplace to determine a need of customers that was not being met, and they met that need in a better way than those that were first to market.

I am not saying there is no advantage to being first to market; there is certainly an advantage, particularly when you cannot protect the invention. But just because something has been done before doesn't mean you can't do it in a better way and see results for that effort.

To analyze your competition, start by writing a list of who your competition is and categorize them as direct or indirect competition.

Take Tesla, for example. Their direct competition would be other EV cars like BYD (Build Your Dream), perhaps. Indirect competition, however, would look like non-EV cars such as Jeep or Holden. Both sell vehicles in the marketplace, and both have competitive analyses to be done.

You want to know how many customers they have, what need is not being met by the competition, and whether you can make those customers yours—or, using my friend as an example, can you make the competition your customer?

Step 4: Financial, Legal, and Technical Feasibility Analysis

Great idea, but I can't see it selling. Great idea, but how are you going to build that? Great idea, but ummm … well, this is awkward … that's slightly illegal.

This step is all about asking, "Is this even feasible?"

You will work out if you can get this idea to market, and what barriers to entry might exist.

There are many reasons your big idea might not be the right big idea right now. People often underestimate their barriers to entry right from the start, and I can tell you this: not only is ignoring barriers to entry the death of a great idea, but it will shut down a company as quickly as you can blink.

CASE STUDY: A few years ago, there was an energy drink that launched here in Australia that had a serious amount of caffeine. The marketing was on point, and it was a dream for my industry where it is helpful, nay, mandatory, to be addicted to caffeine.

No coffee = no workee.

The small issue was the name of the product was illegal. Their marketing was so on point they gave the drink the name of an illegal drug. Great idea … until it wasn't.

It certainly caught my attention. I walked into my regular coffee joint one Friday morning and noticed the new drink, which I was pretty sure was not there the day before. All I could think was to buy it now because it would be off the shelves almost immediately. And yup, by Monday morning, it was gone.

Why was it illegal? Because the name of the drink was also the name of a drug, was misleading and deceptive, and children would not be able to tell the difference between the drink and the real McCoy. In short, it was a dangerous product. ■

That's what you call a barrier to the market under that name. They couldn't sell under that name, but they still had an opportunity to sell under another one. I never found out if they did.

Another barrier may be a substantial investment to fit out a new shop.

Your analysis of the barriers may also identify issues to avoid. In my state, it is illegal to export power outside the property boundary—so no long extension cords for my EV charging idea!

CASE STUDY: Let's identify a hard barrier. This is often the *way* you are doing business rather than the actual business. I have a friend who has terrible luck at picking romantic partners. Her potential partners are either married, in long-term relationships, compulsive liars, just plain psycho, or all of those things combined. She would find out the hard way months into a relationship that she was the "other woman" and later found secret social media pages that revealed the true romantic status of her partner.

Enter Clearview. Clearview provided a service that allowed a person to upload an image of another person to generate a report on the social media images and activity of the person.

However, the way Clearview worked breached Australian privacy laws. Clearview would allow a user to upload an image of the person. It would then convert the image to a faceprint and scour its database of images taken from the internet for a match. Faceprints are biometric data, which are a special kind of personal information. Clearview had a database of images (converted to faceprints) that it had obtained from the social media pages of millions of people around the world.

Clearview was investigated by our Privacy Commissioner for breaches of our *Privacy Act*, and the Commissioner found the method Clearview used to store data and generate reports effectively went too far.

The Privacy Commissioner deemed the action of converting social media images to a faceprint was beyond the reasonable expectation of how those images would be used.

In short, the monetization of a person's personal data was beyond the reasonable expectations of those persons, so the services of Clearview were "unreasonably intrusive and unfair". This case also shows that companies formed in one country can unintentionally infringe laws of other countries if they have not done their due diligence. Clearview was an American company, but it was found to breach Australian privacy laws. ■

The lesson to be learned here is to obtain legal advice

on the way you do business, as that *way* may be a hard barrier to the market.

First, it's essential to look at the regulatory barriers that exist for your product. What licenses, permits, and regulations might hinder market entry?

Next, is economy of scale on your side? Do established competitors benefit from reduced costs due to large-scale production? If you're just starting out and producing lower quantities of product versus your competition, can you afford to compete?

Are you going up against Coca-Cola? Your customers may feel strongly about their loyalty to an established brand, making it hard (nay, almost impossible) to compete as a new entrant.

Sometimes law and economies of scale clash. In my career as a computer programmer, I was lucky enough to work around the world. In particular, in the late 1990s, I was fortunate enough to live and work in England.

I was married with no kids, earning a very nice living coding during the Y2K years. For those who don't know, the Y2K years were a golden time for computer programmers because we were a hot commodity. There was very little unemployment in the industry, and companies paid good money to ensure their systems didn't go down at the strike of midnight when the year changed from 1999 to 2000. It was also a time when computer memory, particularly RAM and hard drives, was very expensive. The cost of digital memory was so bad that a gang of thieves was breaking into companies (including the company I worked for) and stealing RAM (this is relevant, later).

I was having a ball and was involved in a project that was a total replacement of the existing system due to a combination of how old the code was and the threat of the Y2K bug. The Y2K bug was a possible computer error because the date of the computer would roll to be 2000. It was common to use the last two digits of the year in an algorithm. The Y2K bug was effectively a concern that the systems would crash because of a 00 date. This was taken so seriously by some companies that it was rumored that CEOs of airlines were required to take the first flight of the year 2000—in other words, put their life on the line to fix the possible bug.

In researching the "fix" to the Y2K bug for this company, it was decided to develop replacement code with newer coding techniques and coding languages. The old code only ran on one operating system on a single server. The newer code would run on any operating system, enabling them to reduce costs by using cheaper, and importantly, shared servers.

They were to move from a server that was currently located in Germany to a shared server in another European country. This would reduce hosting costs considerably. The trouble was the data held on the German server included personal information. The privacy laws forbade the export of personal information out of Germany. The company in charge of the project didn't know that—they hadn't researched the law.

But here was what killed the project: the cost of memory was so high that the rewrite project, which was to take more memory, was not viable if the servers had to be kept in Germany—it was only viable if the servers were shared. The project reverted to simply fixing the old code to overcome the Y2K bug and the data remained in Germany.

Whilst this isn't exactly a barrier to entry, it was a barrier to the project. This barrier should have been detected before the project was started, not after paying programmers to build a replacement system for nine months.

Step 5: Unique Value Proposition (UVP)

What makes you so special? What are you offering that the others aren't? Is it an invention that is so profound you are first to market, and it changes how people function?

Your unique value proposition (UVP) is your biggest drawing card. It is what makes customers buy from you in the first place and return to you repeatedly.

This is where IP rights come into their own. Having the correct IP rights in place forces customers to buy from you.

But even if you can't secure all the rights you want, you can still dominate your marketplace. It might be that your product lasts longer, is better for the environment, is at a cheaper price point, or creates an emotion.

Let's discuss what drives a sale: emotion. Every sale ever made in the world satisfies an emotion.

To use an example, let's look at wheat flour. There are three brands of wheat flour on the shelves at my local store, each with a distinct price point of low, middle, or high. People buy the lower-priced flour because it is the lowest price point. The emotion they are satisfying is the satisfaction of feeding their family whilst still following a budget and not "wasting" money on the higher-priced flour that is exactly the same flour as what they just bought. People who buy the higher-priced flour don't want to be seen budgeting, they don't want the cheap flour in their trolly. It satisfies the emotion of being seen as being well-to-do. Those who buy the middle-priced flour don't want to be seen with the cheap flour but don't want to waste money.

Each buyer has been driven by emotion.

The same emotions are at play with other types of goods, such as fashion items. Some just HAVE to be seen with the latest Nikes or this season's clothes!

Some people will buy a handbag for the mere fact that the brand is more expensive and more importantly, visible. They want others (often whom they see as being beneath them in social class structures) to see them buying the expensive brand—this is why knockoffs are so popular. People want to be seen as being higher in social structures, and buying that brand displays that they are above others who can't afford that brand. Their emotion is satisfied.

But something odd happens once people believe they have reached a certain level of social class structure. The emotion being met changes. People no longer care about whether those that are *beneath* them see them as being able to afford that brand. Rather, they care about the reaction of people they see as equals. Thus, they buy brands that are more subtle in their branding. Those brands have still satisfied an emotion—but in a different way.

Again, you should be thinking outside the box. If you invented a competing teleporter, could your teleporter be varied so that when it teleports an animal (for example), it does not teleport cancer cells? Perhaps in inventing a competing teleporter, you have also invented a 100 percent effective treatment for cancer without even realizing it. Is a cancer cure your UVP?

So, what is your unique position? What are you selling? Can you protect it from others? See our next chapter for how to protect your winning ideas.

Step 6: SWO(P)T - Identify Opportunities for Protection, Growth Potential, and Trends

Wouldn't it be amazing if we had a crystal ball that would foretell all the issues, growth potential, and trends your product will face before coming (or even after arriving) to market?

If I could invent THAT, I'd be a trillion-aire, my friends.

You knew it was coming. It's essential. If you don't SWOT, you also don't make bank. It's that simple, P.I.T.C.H.ers.

Conducting a SWOT is a *business 101* step. Every serious business should conduct a SWOT.

If you've done all the research, a SWOT puts your proverbial ducks in a row and reveals the pros, cons, and unknowns you need to know before diving in.

Strengths: Why does your idea work? How will it benefit others?

Weaknesses: Where is there room for improvement?

Opportunities: How can you change the industry or product for the better?

Threats: Where are you likely to get into trouble? Where might you need more information?

So many excited, innovative P.I.T.C.H.ers skip this step or think they just "know" it'll be a money-making idea. I get it. And, the fastest way you'll make it a reality, the thing that everyone, from investors to the bank and back again, wants to know is: What does your SWOT say?

It's time to SWOT some sense into your idea.

I like to add one more letter to SWOT, which is 'P' for Positioning. Knowing how your competitors position themselves in the market and how you should position yourself could be the defining factor between standing out or shutting down.

You want to be known for standing out in your marketplace. The only way to do that is to know what positions have already been filled.

We seek to identify what is already in the market and create a solution that is not already in the market—or at least a product that has a unique value to buyers. We look at our legal protections and exclusivity to protect our ideas from competitors. Yes, this is where your legal counsel (still not me!) can advise on what's needed, what's possible, and where to start.

But, we do have some tools we too can access, like historical data and what the past market growth rates have looked like—slow and stagnant or dropping off?

The world moves fast. You need to keep up. Dinosaurs bit the dust for a simple reason: they didn't evolve. But their evolutionary cousins, the crocodiles, adapted and thrived. So, it's time to embrace your inner croc, evolve with the changing world, and do more than just survive—aim to flourish!

What are the opportunities in your industry? Your ability to forecast and predict market growth purely based on data and market trends will give you a leg up when launching your ideas, dear P.I.T.C.H.er.

Want the really good stuff? Macro trending looks at the broader societal, technological, economic, environmental, and political trends that could affect the market. It turns your idea into a winning one by exploring all the angles it could work and why (or why not).

Macro-trending refers to trends in industries (or society, etc) that are predicted to make an impact in the five-to-ten-year period, whilst micro-trending refers to short-term trends.

Identifying a macro-trend allows you to forecast the future of industries so you can plan to meet that need for your clients. In other words, you will predict what your customers want before they want it and plant yourself firmly in that space. Did you ever think you could communicate without wires before Wi-Fi was invented?

CASE STUDY: A micro-trend that emerged during the pandemic was the use of online video meetings to replace in-person, face-to-face meetings. It met an immediate need of not being in the proximity of other humans but still meeting the need for human interaction. At the time, it was considered to be temporary, yet we are still having online video meetings today. Rather than seeing it as a health saver, we now see it as a permanent fixture.

Some saw the future of meetings being online. Prior to the pandemic, they predicted this macro-trend and invested in developing online meeting software. A wonderful example of how this became successful is the story of Zoom. Zoom was already in place before the pandemic, so *during* the pandemic, Zoom's stock price skyrocketed. Did Zoom see a pandemic coming or just get lucky? Who knows, but Zoom was well placed either way. ∎

While many only go surface level with their SWOT, I recommend reviewing a couple of spaces that consistently get overlooked: distribution channels and pricing and revenue models.

Distribution Channels

If, in the past few months or years, you've tried to purchase something from a shop only to find it unavailable, sold out, or back ordered, you already know a thing or two about distribution.

Just look at the toilet paper hoarding of the pandemic era, and you'll see the challenges in desire and distribution.

Distribution is simply how products or services reach the end-user in their market.

Perhaps, in your industry, there are already established distribution channels. Take, for example, Apple products, which are typically only sold at Apple-approved retailers. If you were inventing the next iPod and not formally part of Apple, you could assume that this distribution channel would be closed to you. However, there may be an opportunity to disrupt or even innovate in this area!

You need to identify how you will distribute your products and services. Are you going the traditional retail route, and if so, how will you break into that marketplace? How will you convince retailers to stock your products? Some retailers have buying groups. Some retailers will only buy from specific suppliers in that industry. You need to have that supplier stock your product before the retailers will even see your product.

Are you going to sell online? If so, using what platform? Are you setting up an online store on your own website or selling through Amazon or eBay? Or will you do both?

Consider what distribution channels are open to you.

Pricing and Revenue Models

While we all want to make millions on our ideas, before you start charging mega-bucks, do some research into prevailing pricing strategies in your market.

Take, for example, laundry soap. In many markets, it runs only a few dollars. If you wanted to launch a competing product for triple the market price readily available, it may not make you money. What is your UVP? Why would people pay triple the price for your product?

Likewise, if everyone's selling a new hair dryer for $80 and your product can compete for a fraction of that at, say, $30, you might be able to capitalize (literally) on the reduced price.

This doesn't mean you always have to undercut the competition. On the contrary.

Sometimes, introducing a new higher priced but exclusive or radically better option makes more sense in the marketplace. Would you pay more to use a teleporter that cures cancer than you would pay for one that doesn't? You won't know until you know why others charge what they do and how you can gain the upper hand.

When determining the price point for your product or service, you need to consider not only your costs of getting the product to market and what profit margin you wish to make but also what the market will pay and your value. If the market won't pay what it costs to get the product to market, look at cutting costs, otherwise your business will be short-lived.

Some will try to hit the market at a cost point just above a slim profit. When asked why, traders generally respond with, "Because that's what it's worth." But, dear P.I.T.C.H.er, it isn't about what YOU think it is worth. It is what your customers think it is worth.

Back in my engineering days, I had a friend who worked as a consultant analyst programmer programming WINCE (a type of operating system) machines, which is a very nuanced specialty area. The competitors were charging $120 per hour, but my dear friend was charging $65 per hour. Despite this, he couldn't catch a break. I suggested he put his rates up closer to the competitor's price for three months to test the waters. He couldn't see the sense in upping his fees when he already couldn't catch a break. He was eventually convinced to try it, and he went away seemingly unhappy. We finally caught up about six months later, and he was booked solid for nine months.

The lesson here was that he priced himself based on what he felt he was worth, which wasn't much compared to the competitor. What he didn't understand initially is that the secret is not to value yourself through your own eyes but to value yourself through the eyes of the customer. What does the customer think you or your product is worth? The signal my friend was sending by pricing himself so low was that he wasn't just a cheap option, but he was a cheap option that must not be of value or must not be quality. Once he raised his fees, he was seen as the slightly cheaper alternative, and his customers suddenly saw his worth.

Also, consider different pricing models. What about the subscription model?

Can you make money from data within your industry? Data is the new oil. In our laundry example, if the data is so valuable to the laundromat, could it give its services away for free? <gasp> This would entice more

Airbnb hosts to use the service, thus gaining the laundromat more data to sell as part of its reporting service.

The idea of giving away services is not so strange, and the technique is used successfully in Australia for "flybuys." Flybuys is a loyalty card system whereby you (being a shopper) swipe your Flybuy card at certain outlets to obtain points based on your purchases. The buyer uses the card to collect the points and then spends the points to discount later purchases. The card is free for buyers, even though the buyer gets a discount on later purchases. So how does Flybuys make money after covering the cost of all the discounts? It sells reports based on customer purchases and trends. In this case, the buyer is the resource that is being used. Nothing is free in this life. Consider that when something is given for free; you are the product being sold—or at least your data is.

This technique is not only used for spending data. Shopping centers use it to fix rents. That free Wi-Fi in shopping centers? Well, it is being used to track where you are walking and how long you spend in an area of the shopping center. That data is then used to set leasing prices for the retailers in the shopping center. Each shop will have their rent based on how much *people traffic* passes their doors. Again, you and your data are the commodity being sold here.

In short, it's essential that we, as P.I.T.C.H.ers, learn exactly what customers are willing to pay, how they prefer to pay, and how to use data—the new oil—to smooth our way to success.

Also, consider different payment options. If your customers love credit card purchases, but you don't accept credit card payments, then you will miss out on sales—you have failed to know and meet your customer's needs.

Again, a word of warning on barriers to markets and regulatory compliance: there may be some industries where pricing models, payment techniques, etc., are not permitted. For example, in some countries, you cannot buy gambling products (lotto tickets and the like) by credit.

Competitor Assessment

You ran your own SWOT ... now do it for others. Analyzing your competition puts you head and shoulders above them regarding market placement and viability.

You should be doing frequent competitor assessments throughout your P.I.T.C.H. Method journey and your journey through increasing the maturity of your organization to make sure the idea, timing, and launch are all successful.

What did we learn?

This chapter covered the knowledge you will need for the first analysis of your idea. Does it work? Will it work? Should it work? Essential questions.

Here's a recap of the analysis you need to know:

- Is the idea a viable opportunity?
- What is the size of the marketplace?
- Who are your customers?
- What do your customers want—what pains are they suffering that you are curing?
- Who are your competitors, and what are they selling—what is your value proposition, and why should customers buy your product over the competitor's product?
- Can you protect the idea from competitors?
- What regulations might apply? What other barriers to market are there?
- How will you have the product manufactured, and where are you distributing the product— what are your distribution channels?
- What are you charging, and what is your expected profit?

- What is your SWO(P)T?

A Final Note:

If you want your idea to succeed, your aim in launching it into the world should not be to make a billion dollars. Those who start with money top of mind often find themselves way behind. Instead, your aim should be to solve a problem in the marketplace so that customers will buy your product and favor it over the competitor's product.

You must distinguish yourself in the marketplace from those with an established brand, product, and funnel for sales. Perhaps you are doing that through launching a novel idea, or perhaps by being at a particular price point, by creating a cult following, or by being the only one permitted to sell that converted product so your customers have no choice but to buy from you.

Launching a new idea is genuinely the hardest thing you will ever do. I talk about personality types and the end goal suited to different personality types in later chapters. Some personality types are suited to start-ups and being a founder, and some are not. Choosing an end goal that suits your personality type will determine your success in making money from ideas.

Don't be hard on yourself. People do not become

successful overnight, regardless of the media advertising a person's get-rich-quick story. Also, not all great inventions come in an inspiring lightning bolt. The Commonwealth Scientific and Industrial Research Organisation[3] (CSIRO) is the inventor of some of the technologies used in Wi-Fi. It took the CSIRO years to overcome the problem of reverberation, where in confined spaces radio waves bounce off surfaces, causing the signal to scramble. Don't think your invention is not worthy because you had to spend time to figure it all out.

And, if you've done all your analysis and are still sitting there pondering what on earth to do with an idea so innovative, so new, that nobody understands how it works, you may still have a very viable idea.

Launching a product that changes paradigms of thinking is the hardest of all commercialization routes, but is it worth it? You'll just need to educate the marketplace first on your concept. Educate before profit. Easier said than done.

Only you and your SWO(P)T will tell.

---

3   CSIRO. "Bringing WiFi to the World." CSIRO, n.d. https://www.csiro.au/en/research/technology-space/it/wireless-lan.

CHAPTER THREE

ARMOR UP

(a.k.a. IP IQ)

Idea protection is the act of safeguarding your brainchild, protecting your wisdom. Just like a knight wouldn't charge into a jousting tournament without their trusty armor, you wouldn't release your ingenious ideas into the world without the shield of intellectual property (IP) to fend off pillaging competitors.

Imagine the classic tale of two inventors—Person One and Person Two—and their groundbreaking ideas.

Person One, in all their creative glory, comes up with a game-changing concept but decides not to armor it with IP protection. They reckon, "I'll just pitch my idea to this big player in the market. No need for legal mumbo-jumbo. These are honorable people. They mean no harm." So, they march into the arena with their game-changing idea laid bare, like a knight in his undies.

Now, enter Person Two, savvy and well-prepared. They've got their IP secured, wrapped up tight in the armor of pending patents, trademarks, and all the IP goodies. At the same meeting, they declared proudly, "Behold, my invention. Patents and trademarks protect it!" You can bet it caught the big player's attention.

Person One is in hot water. The big player thinks, "Why bother dealing with this person when I can snatch this idea and run to the hills with it?" No knights in shining armor here, more like knights in ugly woolly socks! Without IP protection, Person One's idea is as defenseless as a sheep in a wolf's den.

Meanwhile, Person Two has set up an intellectual fortress. The big player knows they can't just waltz away with the idea because the law safeguards it. Person Two is in a whole different league. They literally suited up for the occasion.

But it gets even better: IP rights won't just protect you as you search for investors, they will cast a spell on your customers to force them to buy from you and only you.

See, the power of IP protection goes beyond just saving your idea from theft. It's your secret weapon in the business world, your ace up your sleeve. Whether you're selling, licensing, or even just sleeping at night, IP is your trusty sidekick.

In this chapter, I'll unravel the mysteries of how you actually protect your big idea. I'll be delving into patents, trademarks, copyrights, design rights, and trade secrets. To keep you entertained, there will be potions, knights in shining armor, and even trolls.

But here's a word of warning: Each land (or country) has its own set of rules and quirks when it comes to IP. You can't just assume that what works in one land works the same way in another.

Also, don't assume that because you have your intellectual property registered in one country, it will protect you in another. Your magic IP potions won't always spread across the seas.

IP protections can be expensive, but let's think of IP protection as a form of insurance for your brilliant ideas. It might seem costly at first, but just wait until someone tries to run away with your golden eggs.

Speaking of golden eggs, let's take a step back to talk about why you need IP protection and the importance of secrets. Not everyone's cut out to be a golden goose of invention. Some folks out there would rather steal your golden eggs than lay their own. Your natural instinct is to protect your golden eggs by hiding them. But someone may discover those eggs eventually, and by then, it may be too late to protect them.

As an IP wizard, you've got to protect those eggs – your ideas and sometimes your confidential information.

IP Types (a.k.a. the Magic Potion of Invention)

Let's take a quick look at the types of intellectual property.

Intellectual property refers to creations of the mind, such as inventions; literary and artistic Works; designs; and symbols, names, and images.

There are two ways to protect intellectual property. By the laws of the land that expressly protect IP and by contract.

You can protect your IP through contracts, but those magic potions only work against those who agree to be bound.

IP registration provides you with protections under the laws of the land against all the locals (and some foreigners). The catch is that most (but not all) IP rights must be registered to provide you with the protection.

This is where it all gets a bit sticky, I'm afraid. There is not one simple law that protects all intellectual property types; rather, there is a series of laws that protect each different type of intellectual property. It's a bag of magic tricks as opposed to a one-spell-fits-all trick.

Each different type of intellectual property:

- has different protections,
- is obtained in different ways,

- provides protections for different periods,
- is renewable (or not), and
- may even protect you in different places.

Oh, and here's a tip: when it comes to infringement, all of the different types of IP rights have equal weight. They don't trump each other, and there is no one IP right to rule them all.

A defense to infringement of one IP type is not a defense to infringement of the others. A person, the infringer (a.k.a. the opposing party), may infringe one of those different intellectual property rights, some of them, or even all of them. When they infringe all rights, it is somewhat like watching someone falling from the top of a tree and hitting their head on every branch on the way down … each smack, just like each infringement, is going to hurt.

In the world of innovation, our IP magic potions or magic tricks include:

- **Patent Registration:** Patents protect the functionality of something or a method of doing something.
- **Copyright Rights:** Protect various "Works" like literary, artistic, dramatic and musical Works.
- **Designs Rights**, otherwise known as

Industrial Designs: Protect the appearance of things.

- **Trademarks:** Protect words, logos, slogans, sounds, smells, colors and other things that can act as a badge of origin.
- **Trade Secrets:** Protect business secrets (e.g., confidential information).

Patents: Your Golden Ticket to Dominance in Your Marketplace

Buckle up because we're about to plunge headfirst into the thrilling world of patents. That's your ticket to securing your golden eggs and ensuring no one else snatches them away.

A little history for you and the reason I am using medieval terminology: Back in the 1600s, England introduced a law known as the Statute of Monopolies. In a nutshell, it said that nobody gets a monopoly unless they've got a patent—then known as a "letters patent." It granted a monopoly over inventions of "new manufacture" for fourteen years. That means that only the person who owned the patent got to use the invention disclosed in the patent for fourteen years. After the fourteen years had expired, anyone could use the invention. We only lived until we were about thirty-five back in those days; it was equivalent to giving you a monopoly for the rest of your life.

So, what's a patent? It's an official intellectual property right granted by a government that grants the patent holder, known as a patentee (that's the savvy trader—you, hopefully—with the patent), the exclusive right to work their magic with the invention revealed within that patent for a period of time. These days, that is twenty years.

In other words, a patent gives you, and those you authorize, a right to exploit (that's patent speak for manufacture, sell, license, import, use, etc.) the invention in the area. This means your competitors cannot use the invention without permission.

Because you, and only you, can make the product, your customers are forced to buy it from you. This is one of the magic spells of patents, and this is why investors love patents so much. The patent gives the business an exclusivity in the marketplace that no other trader has.

But there's a catch: to obtain a patent, you must spill the beans on how your invention works. You can't keep it a secret.

It's a bit like striking a deal with the government, saying, "I'll show you how this fantastic invention works, and in return, I get the exclusive right to use it for a period of time."

And you can't be sneaky about it by holding back the magic. If you don't "disclose" your invention fully, you might just lose your patent rights. Disclosing the invention means you have to describe the invention in the patent document with enough information to allow a person, who normally builds those kinds of things, to build your invention. In patent speak, it's an "enabling disclosure."

If you continue with the process, eventually, your patent will be published on a public register so others can see your secret sauce and, therefore, know not to try to make that same sauce. Just like Jack and his magic beanstalk, it will be noticed.

The concept behind patents is this: creating new inventions demands time, resources, and the brilliance of inventors. As such, inventors deserve a reward for their effort—but only if they're willing to reveal the secret sauce for others to learn from and use after the patent's curtain call.

Picture this: The hallmark of a patent is that the invention is groundbreaking and inventive from the very moment it's first filed. This moment is known as the priority date. Think of it like the land grabs in the 1800s, where folks planted their flags to claim their turf. Filing a patent is like planting your flag in the sand, staking your claim from that day forward.

The priority date is a make-or-break date because it's when your invention goes through the wringer to see if it's truly novel and inventive.

And when I say it is laying a claim, it literally is. A patent comprises a series of "claims" that set out the boundaries of your invention. Consider them your castle walls that define your rights.

Before your patent is granted, it will be examined to ensure it is new and inventive compared to all similar inventions that existed at the priority date. Those prior things are known as "prior art." If your invention isn't up to snuff (if it is not novel or inventive) compared to the prior art, it won't get registered.

But you aren't out of the woods even then. Even if your patent is registered, other people can challenge it if they claim it was not up to snuff.

This technique is a not-so-secret weapon to fight off an allegation that you have infringed a patent. If you are accused of infringing a patent, you would bring out the big guns with a counterclaim (in the boxing ring, that's a return punch) to declare the patent invalid. And, if the patent is invalid (i.e., it should not have been granted in the first place), you can't have infringed it. And that's a knockout punch in the boxing ring.

But be careful because the law applies to you just as much as it applies to others—be sure not to knock yourself out of the game. If you disclose[4] your invention before you file it (i.e., before your priority date), it won't be novel or inventive at its priority date, and you will have knocked yourself out and scored an own goal.

I get it. You are a wheeler and a dealer. You've got places to be and people to see. You need to disclose your invention to get some deals in place. So, how do you protect yourself before you file the patent? You'll need a non-disclosure agreement. I talk about those below.

Patents are a gift that keeps on giving. Experienced business people know how to play the patent game and understand the power of patents. Patents are like secret weapons for marketplace domination. The key is to keep inventing as your competition is playing catch-up.

Imagine being in a league of your own, where your patented inventions give you an 80 percent stranglehold on the market. You know the competition's lurking, so you keep innovating. The day they come close, you unleash your new masterpiece and file a new patent application. Suddenly, your customers can't get enough of your new superior, efficient, *you-name-it* product. Your rivals are still playing catch-up, and you're in the lead again (*hint*: think Apple). The beauty of

---

4   Truth be told, a number of countries have a grace period where you can use your patent for a period of time prior to filing. But it is a dangerous game. Use before you file in one country can invalidate your rights in countries that don't have a grace period. Avoid using the grace period if you can, but if you can't some protection is better than nothing.

this strategy is that you can market your new product to your existing customers as the next big thing. You've already claimed your territory and established your dominance.

This is the power of patenting.

Of course, it is not that simple. Not everything is patentable. Remember that in the 1600s, only things that were a *new manufacture* were patentable. The term used now is *manner of manufacture*, and what that is varies worldwide, but it generally means that the invention:

- has to be useful and inventive,
- cannot be an abstract idea, a scientific principle, or an artistic creation,
- must be an invention, not a discovery.

The tests of what is patentable changes as courts make decisions on what is and is not patentable. Remember our CSIRO example? Well the CSIRO patented part of the technology used in Wi-Fi which is software running on hardware. Based on today's tests of what is or is not patentable in my country, it is unlikely to be patentable.

With advancements in Artificial Intelligence, the question has been raised as to whether an AI can be listed as an inventor for the purposes of a patent. There is no question that AI can invent, but can AI be the inventor for a patent. Remember the nature of the bargain for monopoly rights is that you have to disclose the invention.

DABUS[5] is the name given to an AI created by Dr Thaler. DABUS stands for "Device for the Autonomous Bootstrapping of Unified Sentience." DABUS is essentially a computer system that's been programmed to invent on its own.

Dr Thaler filed patents naming DABUS itself as the inventor … and, well, that started the fight. To date, the question of whether DABUS (or AI) can be an inventor under the various patent acts around the world has been heard in at least the United States, Australia, New Zealand and Europe and the resounding answer is NO. The only hold out to this position is South Africa, but that is because there was no substantial examination process—so watch this space.

5   Wikipedia contributors. "DABUS." Wikipedia, February 21, 2024. https://en.wikipedia.org/wiki/DABUS.

ProTip: Always list the correct inventor names on patent applications—in some countries, listing the wrong names, or missing names, can render a patent invalid. Always use a qualified and registered patent agent to draft and file patent applications. The stakes are too high to trust those who don't know what they are doing.

In the past few years, there has been some uproar regarding gene patenting. This kicked up when a company invented a way of extracting the breast cancer gene. People lost their minds, claiming that we weren't allowed to have babies anymore because if we made babies with the breast cancer gene, we'd infringe the patent. *Let's all calm down a little—feel free to procreate.* The courts in Australia and the United States, as well as many other countries, decided that genes were discoveries and, therefore, not patentable.

Why else would you patent?

Not every inventor wants to end up in the boxing ring. Most would prefer to avoid it. But they still choose to patent their inventions. And for good reason.

1. **Investors LOVE patents:** If you want to attract investors, a good way to do so is by getting your patents in place as soon as possible. Patents increase the chances that an investor will recoup their investment. By holding exclusive rights, there may be an opportunity to charge premium prices, which results in higher profit margins.

2. **Licensing potential = more revenue:** Licensing a patent to others can be a huge source of revenue for inventors who either don't want to or don't have the capacity to manufacture the invention.

3. **Higher valuation:** Patents can significantly boost a company's valuation and paint a picture larger than just the current profit and loss statement. Patents are often viewed as a sign of innovation and market advantage, making the business more attractive to investors, partners, or potential buyers.

4. **Fostering innovation via knowledge sharing:** Because the patent system requires public disclosure of patented inventions, it fosters and encourages innovation and development in the respective field. Think of the *communal mind*; sharing knowledge advances us all.

5. **Tax-friendly:** In some jurisdictions, patents can qualify for tax cuts on income, either on the

income derived from the patent itself or through additional deductions for research and development expenses related to the patented invention.

6. **Grant-friendly:** Holding a patent or having a patent pending can enhance eligibility for government or private research grants. These grants are often aimed at promoting scientific and technological innovation, and having a patent demonstrates a commitment to these goals.

7. **Patents are protection:** Patents are a layer of protection against those who seek to steal or profit off of your hard work. The threat of legal action for patent infringement can be a powerful tool in protecting a company's market share. This aspect of patents can prevent competitors from encroaching on patented technology or products, even if actual litigation is not pursued.

8. **Leverage when you need it:** If you find yourself in a dispute or are negotiating a deal, patents give you more leverage to work with. They are often used as bargaining chips in licensing discussions or cross-licensing agreements.

What Do Patentees and Sorcerers Have in Common?

Quite a bit, actually. There's a fair bit of money in patent litigation. Like a cunning sorcerer lying in wait, some patentees bide their time, concealing themselves, waiting for an unsuspecting person to strike it rich by unknowingly infringing the patent. That's when the patent owner (the sorcerer) unleashes their legal spells to claim a share of the gold coins the infringer holds.

It all seems like harmless fun and magic tricks until you find yourself the target of such a magical assault.

Speaking of magical exceptions, remember when the crown was the highest ruler of them all? Numerous countries possess a unique "crown law" exception that applies to patents.

In the early 1900s, when world wars raged on, governments needed the power to wield any weapon, including patented ones, for the protection of their people in times of war, without the worry of being refused access. Hence, they crafted the "crown law" exception, granting governments the right to exploit a patent, almost like a compelled, non-free license. However, even in the world of magic, there's no such thing as a free lunch, and the government is still required to pay a fair price for its patent (in most countries).

Remarkably, often the laws do not specify that the crown law exception is solely for times of war. So, every once in a while, the government might conjure up a license for rather mundane things, such as electricity meters, or they may even dabble in a bit of IP infringement until they are caught, at which point, they assert their crown law rights. On a more serious note, I would expect the crown law exception to be fully exploited if there was a medicine that would save people from another pandemic. And *some* countries have this exception in their *Patents Act*; the government can freely and, sometimes, without cost use medicines to save its citizens.

Some patents remain shrouded in secrecy. These patents, often related to national security matters, may never see the light of day.

Patent Myths Debunked

Myth: You can patent any idea or invention.

Debunked: To be patentable, an invention must be new, non-obvious, and useful, amongst other things. Ideas that are purely abstract, natural phenomena, or illegal are not patentable.

Myth: Patents protect your invention across the globe.

Debunked: There are different laws in different lands. Protection in one country does not guarantee protection in another. Patents are territorial and require that the inventor apply for patents in every country where they want to be protected.

Myth: Patents last forever.

Debunked: Patents expire. They typically provide protection for twenty years from the filing date, after which the invention enters the public domain. Maintenance fees are also payable, so if you don't pay the fee the patent will lapse.

Myth: Patents guarantee commercial success.

Debunked: There are no guarantees for success, but there are business tools that increase your odds of success, and patents are a business tool.

What it does do is give you the right to exclude others from making, using, selling, or importing your invention.

Myth: The first to invent always gets the patent.

Debunked: Actually, most countries operate on a 'first to file' system (not a first to invent system). So if you're the first inventor to file an application for an invention, you're more likely going to be granted the patent, regardless of whether other inventors are involved.

Myth: I can sell my product in other countries even if I don't have a patent in those other countries.

Debunked: Again, patents are largely territorial. Just because you have rights in the country you manufactured your product in, it's possible to infringe a patent in another country by exporting your product into that country. There are other ways you may accidentally infringe a patent in another country. Just another reason to file patent applications wherever you want to protect your invention, increase profit, avoid litigation, and eliminate any barriers that could limit your sales potential.

ProTip: If you let someone, such as a distributor, use your patent (known as the licensee), make sure you own the trademark they use when promoting the patented product (or design, or copyright … you get the drift). Why? Because people buy products based on the name—the trademark. If you part ways with your distributor and trust us, you will eventually, the distributor must start again with a new name and build a reputation in that new name, which is a costly, time-consuming headache to deal with. Meanwhile, you continue with name recognition, reputation, and all the power. Holding the trademark puts you in the driver's seat and makes it easy to find a new distributor because the brand already has a stellar reputation. It's a win-win. For you, at least. That's how you hold all the cards in this game of innovation and ownership.

Copyright Rights and the Copycats

Copyright rights protect the expression of an idea, not

the idea itself. Copyright rights protect various "Works" like literary, artistic, dramatic, and musical Works.

In the simplest terms, "copyright" means "the right to copy," but it also extends to other acts such as creating adaptations, publicizing the Work, and displaying the Work to the public. What it doesn't protect against is independent creation. This means we can write a story about a cat on a mat without stealing it from another, and neither can enforce it against the other. This is relevant in the boxing ring.

Copyright rights are magical in a way because they do not require registration. Rather, the right is created upon the creation of the Work. There's no need to register your magic spell for it to exist. But as a trap for young players, in some countries, you must register your copyright rights to enforce them.

The magic continues. Copyright spells, unlike some others, can travel across lands, depending on where you live. This means copyright rights from one country can be enforced in other countries. If you are lucky enough to be in a Berne Convention country (and given there are 176 Berne Convention countries, it's likely you are), you are provided "national treatment" in the other Berne Convention countries. That means you are treated just like a national of those countries, and whatever law applies to the locals applies equally to you.

This comes as a rather rude shock to the other party sometimes. Their response to infringement allegations is, "But I stole it from [insert the name of another country] and the owner doesn't even use it here, so it doesn't matter." Ah, but it does matter. And your opponent just admitted to the infringement. Oops.

One of my most perplexing bouts in the boxing ring was a logo creation where the logo was incredibly complex. This was not a simple logo. My client unfortunately received a very strongly worded letter from another Berne convention country. The logos were identical and there was no way these two logos could have been developed independently.

That was how the fight started, and oh, it was vicious.

It was clear their lawyer was going all out, and so were we. We served what we thought was our knockout punch, our evidence of independent creation—our drafts, our sketches, our *you-name-it*. They, unfortunately also gave us their evidence that showed how they independently created the logo.

An immediate end to the round was called where we all took time to shake our heads at the coincidence that two wonderfully creative people could devise an almost identical logo at the same time, independently of each other. We were all left to lick our respective wounds.

You've probably seen copyright battles in the media involving some talented famous songstress allegedly stealing the lyrics or score from another equally famous and talented songstress. You know you've hit the big-time when a famous musician accuses you of copyright rights infringement!

You've probably noticed from those cases that when infringement is found, only a tiny bit of the original work was taken. The reason is this. To infringe copyright rights you just need to take a substantial part of the original. But the term substantial is not about size, its about quality—think of it as being quality over quantity. So that is how these songs are said to infringe copyright rights where only a small portion is taken.

One of the problems with these musical cases (well, all copyright cases) is the issue of independent creation. With so many famous and fabulous musicians, double creation is highly likely. And as we saw from our logo example above, artistic works can be complex and can still be created independently by two separate people. No point in crying over spilt milk.

Copyright rights last for a long period of time. These days, in most countries, that time is the life of the author plus 70 years. This means the estate can protect copyright rights for 70 years after the death of the author.

But the law has not always stated the period is 70 years, it was previously a shorter period. Also some creations are so important to the country it will pass special laws to protect those laws.

Mickey Mouse is entering the "public domain". What that means is that the copyright rights in the earlier versions of Mickey Mouse have just expired.

American law allowed copyright rights in Mickey to be held for 95 years after US Congress expanded it several times during Mickey's life.

Mickey's first screen release was in the 1928 short film Steamboat Willie. It is that copyright that has expired, not all the other Mickey Mouse productions.

Don't be fooled into thinking you can steal all things Mickey—you can't. There are many forms and variations of Mickey and copyright rights likely still apply. Tread carefully dear P.I.T.C.H.ers.

Most of the *Copyright Acts* around the world require that the Work is an original creation of a human. So this generally rules out AI owning the images it creates.

Remember the monkey photo saga?[6] British wildlife photographer David J. Slater set up his camera

---

6   Wikipedia contributors. "Monkey Selfie Copyright Dispute." Wikipedia, February 21, 2024. https://en.wikipedia.org/wiki/Monkey_selfie_copyright_dispute.

to take a photo. A wild macaque thought he could do a better job and stole the camera. He closed the shutter thereby taking an adorable "monkey selfie". It was cute and got the world's attention. The trouble came when Mr Slater tried to enforce copyright rights in the monkey selfie. Now remember the macaque was wild, so People for the Ethical Treatment of Animals (PETA), argued that the copyright should be owned by or assigned to the macaque.

Remember that photography is a work of art and setting up the equipment plays a big part in the appearance of a photograph. Surely the human that contributed in such an important way would own some copyright rights in the photograph? That was part of the argument.

Ultimately the US court found that animals have no legal authority to hold copyright claims.

A huge warning about copyright rights. Sometimes you don't own what you created. In some lands, if you pay someone to create something for you, you own that thing and the rights in it. In others you don't. In some countries if an employee creates something for you, you own it, but if a contractor creates it for you, you don't own it (unless you put it in writing that you do). This is one of the biggest issues I face in mergers and acquisitions. Shoddy contracting has been used and to the shock of the buyer and the vendor, the vendor doesn't own what they think they own—and thus the price to be paid plummets.

Now don't panic dear P.I.T.C.H.ers, see my comment below about implied licenses.

> **Aussie ProTip:** Sometimes, different rights overlap each other. If you don't register your rights, you might lose the ability to enforce another right. Copyright rights and design rights overlap in Australia. For most things, if you *could* have registered your design right but *didn't*, you can't rely on copyright rights for the same thing. Why? Because copyright rights are free, but design rights aren't.

Copyright Myths Debunked

Myth: Anything on the internet is in the public domain and free to use.

Debunked: Copyright rights and confidentiality are not the same thing. Just because it's public, doesn't mean you can copy it. Copyright protects original Works of authorship, regardless of where the Work is published or whether the Work is published online or offline.

Myth: If it doesn't have a copyright notice, the Work is free to use.

Debunked: Most modern copyright laws do not require a Work to bear a copyright notice for protection. However, copyright markings are recommended as they put the world on notice the Work is protected and can make infringement proceedings much cheaper to run.

Myth: I don't make a profit from use of the image, so I don't infringe copyright rights.

Debunked: Infringement can occur, whether a profit is made or not.

Copyright Myths Debunked (cont'd)

Myth: If I copy less than 10 percent it does not infringe copyright rights.

Debunked: This is a common myth that is fundamentally untrue for the majority of cases. The test of infringement is whether a substantial amount is taken. Substantiality is a test of quality not quantity. Then the assessment turns to whether a defense applies. So yes, you can still infringe a Work by taking even just a small part.

Myth: You can use copyrighted Works without permission if you credit the source.

Debunked: Crediting the source does not substitute for obtaining permission. Some defenses do apply if the Work is credited, but do not assume these defenses will apply in all situations.

Myth: Changing a Work by 20 percent makes it a new Work.

Debunked: Again, this is not correct. Work derived from another Work may infringe copyright rights.

Trademarks and Trolls

A trademark is *something* that acts as a badge of origin. If people see that *something* and think of you, that *something* acts as a trademark. That *something* can be:

- a logo (which, in the IP trade, is called a device),
- a slogan,
- a name,
- a color,
- and even a scent.

And that's not a complete list.

Unlike patents, trademarks don't need to be novel or inventive to be registered. But in most countries, the mark will be examined against other registered trademarks to ensure it can act as a unique badge of origin for the desired goods and services. This means that if the mark is too close to other marks for similar or identical goods and services, it won't be registered (or at least won't without a fight).

For the purposes of trademark registration, in most countries goods and services are classified into forty-five classes. When you file your application, you designate which classes you want and put your goods and services in the appropriate classes. Your protection is based on your mark and "statement of goods and services," which is a legal way of saying your list of goods and services. Fees are payable on each class for each trademark. Some countries charge extra for longer statements of goods and services. Don't try to be too clever P.I.T.C.H.ers and put all your goods and services into the one class to avoid fees. Your trademark application will be examined by the IP office for "formalities" and if you have goods and services in the wrong class you will have to move them or delete them.

Trademarks are a bit like a donut. The middle of the donut covers you for exactly your mark and the goods and services of your registration. The yummy bit of the donut protects you from marks that are deceptively similar or substantially identical for goods and services that are identical, similar, or of the same description (or whatever terms are used in your country).

In some countries, to file a trademark, you don't even need to be the original user of the trademark. This is a trap for new players.

When you file a trademark application, most IP offices will examine it to ensure that it is not too similar to other marks on the register. It will also examine it to make sure it is registerable as a trademark.

Also, not everything is trademarkable. A trademark needs to act as a badge of origin to identify one trader over another. No one trader can own the trademark APPLE for apples, because it is descriptive, and no matter how much the local fruit store uses the term, it can never distinguish them from other fruit stores. But back in the day, it was pretty unique for a computer company.

Trademarks are registered for a period of ten years and can be renewed indefinitely with payment of the fees. However, trademarks can be removed from the register if they are unused, making trademarks a use-it-or-lose-it regime. Sometimes, that is done by another trader wanting your trademark removed, but in some countries, the official IP office requires that you prove use of your mark, and if you don't, it will be removed from the register, or the unused goods/services will be removed. *I'm looking at you, United States.*

Trademarks only work in the jurisdiction they are registered within. But this is a trap and lulls traders into a false sense of security. Imagine if you had your trademark registered with your local IP office and you are happily selling online. You suddenly get a large order from another country and you think, "This is it, I have finally made it internationally". But what happens if the trademark you are using is owned by another trader in that other country? You might find yourself falling afoul of overseas laws. You see, selling in one country for import into another country can be trademark (or any other type of IP) infringement in that other country.

Tread carefully. The lesson to be learned here is to register your trademark in all the countries in which you want to sell your goods/services or manufacture them under that trademark.

Sometimes marketers (i.e., IP magicians) have done such a stellar job of advertising that people start using the brand name to describe the *thing* they are referring to without even knowing they are using a brand name. They use the brand name as a noun or a verb.

This is a trap for brand owners as they have lost control over the trademark, and the trademark may have become descriptive through use. In these cases, if a trademark has become descriptive after it has been filed, it can be removed from the trademark register because it no longer operates as a badge of origin.

Some brand owners take active steps to beg consumers not to use their trademark in a descriptive manner.

Take Velcro®[7], for instance. Did you know that Velcro is a fastener that should be referred to as being hook and loop? Watch the lawyers of Velcro beg

---

7   VELCRO® Brand. "Don't Say Velcro." Video. YouTube, September 25, 2017. https://www.youtube.com/watch?v=rRi8LptvFZY.

people to refer to their product as "hook and loop" on YouTube. Just search for Velcro.

> **ProTip:** In some countries, there is an overlap between the *Trademarks Act* and the *Patents Act*. If a patented product has been sold under that trademark and nothing else has been sold under that trademark, the trademark owner loses the ability to enforce the trademark after the patent's final curtain. That is to stop patentees from trying to lengthen the life of a patent beyond its term through threatened trademark infringement.

First to Use v First to File (a.k.a. Tell Me about the Trolls)

Buckle up, and let's learn about trolls. Since the dawn of trademarks, there have been trolls. I'm not talking about online trolls, I'm talking about those weasel-like grotesque little things that stink, are infinitely objectionable, and guard bridges and make you pay the toll to pass. Having worked with international trademarks for so long, I am familiar with trolls. Sadly, they're not just a figment of Nordic imagination. In fact, dear

P.I.T.C.H.ers, they exist amongst us, camouflaged to hide their true intentions.

Let me tell you about the trolls.

In the trademark world, there are two types of countries. The first type (and the vast majority) are *first-to-file* countries. In a first-to-file country, you don't need to be the original user of the trademark or even consider yourself the owner to file the mark. If you file the trademark application before anyone else, your local IP office will grant you the trademark if every other test is passed. Even if someone has been using the mark in the country for decades, it's "too bad, so sad" for them because you filed first.

The other type of country is a first-to-use country. In these countries, the first user of the trademark (normally) has the ultimate right of ownership over the trademark. If someone else applies to register the trademark first, the "first user" can oppose the application based on their first-use right. And it gets better: if you are a "first user" and someone manages to score the trademark first, your position as a first continual user is a full defense to infringement, a.k.a. a knockout blow in the boxing ring.

So, back to the trolls.

People know their own local laws. Say you have a famous brand and look like you have money, but you have no protection in a first-to-file country. Well, a trademark troll will notice you have no protection in that country, will then file for the trademark, and try to extort you by offering to sell the trademark in exchange for a king's ransom. Or they will demand an exorbitant license fee for you to be able to continue doing what you have doing for decades.

You might think you should have protected yourself and filed the trademark first, but with so many famous marks, you have to make budget choices. And sometimes, choices backfire.

This happens all the time. It is wrong to refer to these people as trolls. They aren't trolls at all. They are merely using their local laws to their advantage, just as we use our local laws to our advantage. This is known as sharp business practices.

Sometimes this works well for the troll but sometimes it doesn't. Remember, we have a bag full of legal IP magic potions, and there are many ways to banish pesky trolls from the kingdom.

Some intellectual property owners continually have to deal with trolls. The pesky things are everywhere. But some trolls aren't always as clever as they think they are. You see, dear P.I.T.C.H.ers, laws go both ways: if the troll wants to rely on local laws, well, so can you and I …

Imagine if a troll targets you and files a trademark for your logo in a country before you have the chance to do so, and then they try to extort you to either pay a license fee or for you to buy the trademark off the troll!

Now imagine you own the copyright rights to the logo.

Remember the rule about being able to enforce copyright rights in Berne Convention countries? Well, in many of the cases I have dealt with, guess where Mr. Troll lived?

So you could send Mr. Troll a strongly worded letter effectively stating, in very polite language, that if he were to use the logo, you'd sue him down to his undies (well kinda, but not really) for copyright rights infringement. And you mean it!

Now let's imagine the letter worked and Mr. Troll never uses the logo.

You decide that this tale is not over. You still want your trademark, and revenge is best served cold.

Remember, trademark rights are a use-it-or-lose-it regime. So, as soon as you can, file a non-use removal application and remove Mr. Troll's trademark from the register. In short, you can combine laws to cast Mr. Troll out the castle walls in his undies (again, kinda, but not really).

Dear P.I.T.C.H.ers, the boxing ring has many

bouts. It isn't a sprint, it's a marathon, and I don't tire easily … and you shouldn't be prepared to, either.

The lesson to be learned here is to protect your trademark in all the countries in which you wish to sell your goods or services. Also try to protect your manufacturing countries, because if a trademark troll registers your trademark in a manufacturing country that is also a first-to-file country, you may have to move your manufacturing to another more expensive country.

* * *

In Australia, Burger King (or Hungry Jacks as it is known here) just won a case brought by McDonalds on the issue of whether a mark should have been registered.

In short, sneaky Hungry Jacks registered BIG JACK as a trademark for burgers etc. McDonald's did not oppose registration of the trademark during the opposition phase and so the trademark was registered.[8]

But McDonalds was none too happy about that and took Hungry Jacks to court to try to cancel the trademark. Ultimately the trademark was not canceled.

The lesson here is—always watch the public trademark registers to see if your competitors are trying to register marks similar to yours. It's easier and more

---

8   https://jade.io/article/1054100

cost efficient to oppose registration of a trademark before it becomes registered than it is to go to court for cancellation after it has become registered.

Savvy traders also know to "watch" the trademark registers to see what their competitors are up to and even get a headstart on what they are about to launch.

ProTip: The purpose of a well-crafted "cease and desist" letter is to cause the receiver to consider whether they have legal exposure in a matter and for them to consider whether they should comply with the demands. The purpose is not to intimidate or make unsubstantiated claims or outlandish demands. You want the other person to accept the offer of settlement and be able to comply with the demands. When outlandish demands are made, it makes the person making the demands appear unreasonable, and the person on the receiving end of the demands may simply do nothing because they either can't comply with the demands or they simply think the demands are disproportionate to the alleged bad acts.

Trademark Myths Debunked

Myth: A trademark is just a company logo.

Debunked: A trademark can be a word, phrase, symbol, design, or a combination of these, used to identify and distinguish goods or services. It's not limited to logos.

Myth: Registering a domain name is enough for trademark protection.

Debunked: Domain registration does not confer trademark rights. Trademark rights are acquired through registration with the appropriate governmental body or through use in commerce (in some countries).

Myth: Trademark rights are global.

Debunked: Like patents, trademark rights are territorial. A trademark registered in one country does not protect the brand in other countries. You can infringe trademark rights in one country by exporting goods into that country and by other actions.

Myth: You can't trademark a color.

Debunked: Colors can be trademarked if they distinctly identify the brand. For example, Tiffany Blue is a registered trademark of Tiffany & Co.

> **Trademark Myths Debunked (cont'd)**
> **Myth:** Once you have a trademark, it lasts forever.
> **Debunked:** Trademark registration is not perpetual. It must be renewed periodically, usually every 10 years. Trademarks can be removed for non-use in most countries, or canceled.

Design Rights/Industrial Designs, and Shiny New Armor

A design right protects the appearance of a thing—the ornamental or aesthetic aspect of an article. Have you created a new cup or pen, bed, or suit of armor? Anything?

To register a design right, it needs to be new and distinctive the day you file it. And yep, that's known as a priority date as well.

Some countries have a grace period whereby you can publicize your design before you file it. (Still, a word of warning there—not all countries have this exception, so publicizing the design before filing it can be fatal to any attempt to register in other countries.)

Unfortunately, designs are registered for a limited

period of time. In my country that is ten years, but in others it is much longer.

That upsets some folks, and they try to work the system by registering their design as a trademark. This technique is ingenious.

Until it isn't. Because trademarks are a use-or-lose-it regime, a trademark must be used *as a trademark* to defeat a non-use removal application. That means you need to use a trademark as a badge of origin. Sometimes, that's hard to do when your design is just a design. Some companies manage to pull this off well. Many drink manufactures protect the shape of their bottles through trademarking. But be warned, not all are worthy and, thus, can not pull this magic trick off. Also, be warned, that appearances can be an odd thing. The smallest of differences can make a huge impact.

Imagine if you created a mirror image of an already existing design. It would materially change how you saw the item, but it was identical to the original design if you held it up to a mirror. An ingenious technique and it shows how a small change can complicate a design infringement case.

Design Myths Debunked

Myth: Industrial design rights protect the way a product works.

Debunked: The functionality of a product is typically protected under patent law. Industrial design rights protect the appearance of a product, not its functional or technical features.

Myth: Design rights are automatically granted upon creation.

Debunked: In many jurisdictions, design rights require registration to provide enforceable protection.

Myth: Design rights are a secondary right.

Debunked: Industrial design rights are a key part of a comprehensive IP strategy, particularly in industries where product differentiation based on design is a critical factor in consumer decision making.

Myth: Design patents and utility patents are the same.

Debunked: Design patents (or industrial designs) protect the appearance of a product, while utility patents protect the functional aspects of an invention.

> **Myth:** Design rights give worldwide protection.
> **Debunked:** Like other IP rights, design rights are territorial and must be registered in each country where protection is sought. You can infringe rights in other countries by selling into that country and by other actions.

What Do Patents, Designs, and Shiny Armor Have in Common?

Designs have received a bad rap previously and are unfairly considered a secondary right. They are the bridesmaids of the IP world—just as powerful and but somehow (and for no good reason) considered the second best.

Patents are like shiny, new, very expensive armor. When they are new and shiny, you don't want to risk scratching your new armor or, worse, writing it off.

What if someone infringed your patent, but you didn't want to take it into battle in case it got slashed to pieces (i.e., declared invalid in a cross-claim)? Wouldn't it be great if you could have a sacrificial lamb instead? Enter the design bridesmaid.

Combining design rights with patent rights is a

great technique for splitting risk. If you have a great invention that looks a certain way, and your enemy makes something that looks identical, but you don't want to risk a cross-claim against your patent, you can run a design infringement case without risking the patent.

You should always register a design associated with your patent because the enemy may make something that looks identical to your patented product but does not infringe on the patent. The design would be the armor you'd take into battle.

Trade Secrets, Confidential Information, and KFC (a.k.a. the Not-So-Secret Herbs and Spices)

You've learned about registrable IP rights and what can and cannot be registered. But there are some ideas or inventions that just can't be protected by IP registrations. So what do you do?

There are other provisions you might be able to rely upon, but they should not be your favored protection because they are uncertain and can be tricky to enforce. Those rights are rights in the area of trade secrets and confidential information.

Let's move on from trolls and talk about snitches. People are snitches: willingly or unwillingly sharing information to get ahead. And just like trolls, they are everywhere. Half the problem is snitches don't know they are snitches. People don't know what they don't know. They don't know what is confidential and what is not.

People are inherently terrible at keeping secrets. Even when they know it's a secret, it eats them alive. Some of them burst with excitement.

There was once a TV show called Veronica's Closet. In one episode, the competitor beat them to get new lingerie designs into the marketplace, and the company could not work out the source of the leak. It turns out that a secretary was doodling on plain wrapping paper before wrapping gifts, thus revealing the new designs for all to see. A television show may be make-believe, but let me tell you, dear P.I.T.C.H.ers, that example is as real as it gets.

When your company is launching a new exciting product, don't chat to the bus driver about it, or the Uber driver, or doodle your designs on wrapping paper. Spilling secrets happens at all levels of a company. We know that IP battles aren't just about whispers behind closed doors; sometimes, it's an all-out war in the boardroom. Directors are trying to pilfer secrets or steal away customers. It's like *Game of Thrones* with non-disclosure agreements.

The problem with secrets is they don't stay that way forever. As technologies evolve, we can determine secrets. The software can be reverse-engineered, people talk, companies are hacked, and even Colonel Sanders' eleven herbs and spices have been reverse-engineered. Secrets don't stay secret forever.

Trade secrets are a company's confidential information. It is information that is proprietary to a company, protected by that company, and is secret. It could be a way of securing two bits of wood together, or the method the company used to overcome a programming issue it was facing, or even what products it was about to launch.

In one of the worst cases I have ever heard of, two lawyers were on a plane chatting away and discussing litigation. They were discussing the strategies that would be used and what the case would entail. Little did they know that sitting behind them was the CEO of their client. He got off the plane and stormed into the legal offices, yanking the file and taking it to a more discrete competitor. And rightly so. You don't know who is around you and who is listening in. Revealing that confidential information forced the client to adopt a different litigation strategy entirely and almost derailed the case.

Some countries have *Trade Secret Acts* that

specifically protect trade secrets. *I'm looking at you United States*. But for those who don't, we rely on non-disclosure agreements (NDAs), other contracts, and other laws that have evolved to protect confidential information.

It's an unspoken rule in the corporate world: every company has the sacred right to shield its confidential intel. That means you can protect yourself against others using your confidential information, but only to the extent that it is confidential. The information must be confidential in nature.

Once you make it public, such as by selling your goods with the previously confidential formula, you've snitched on yourself—the horses have bolted, and you can't close the gates. The geese have flown and are laying golden eggs in the wrong places.

If you can go about your business and sell your goods without snitching on yourself or having someone snitch on you, that's all well and good. But the rest of us mere humans need to get on with business, and that means telling people our secrets so that we can partner with them, sell to them, or even pitch to them.

So, how do you protect your trade secrets?

Remember the sales pitch by Person One, who pitched with no protection at all, and Person Two, who suited up for the occasion? Well, Person Two contacted the big players before they walked into the room and had them sign a non-disclosure agreement.

Person Two had done this before and made sure that NDA bound the big player so the big player couldn't disclose his secrets to others, and the big player wouldn't use the secrets internally to the detriment of Person Two. The big player also agreed that if they get to chatting and the big player contributes to the idea, then even though the big player has contributed, Person Two still owns all rights to the idea. This was a master stroke because it stopped the big player from later claiming ownership of the patent or idea just because it had suggested a few things.

Under NDAs, the deal is simple: you reveal your secrets, and the other party promises not to tell your secrets to anyone else or use your secrets against you.

But NDAs have an Achilles heel. If the information stops being confidential, it isn't protected under the NDA.

How does that work with patents, designs, and trademarks that appear on IP registers and are declared to the world? If your product's functionality is your golden egg, patenting is like shouting it from the rooftop.

And how does that work when you want to pitch your ideas if they aren't patentable?

Simple! First, you start with an NDA with all the bells and whistles that protect your IP. This allows you to approach others to discuss your idea with them confidentially. It doesn't destroy novelty in your invention because it's all on the down-low.

After discussing the idea, you either break up or move on to another phase.

You need to enter into another agreement that sets down the rules of play for the next stage of your relationship. It might be an agreement to make a prototype, develop software, or a widget, or something. This agreement should make it clear who owns the IP in whatever is created. And since I'm on your side here (but still not your lawyer), I'd prefer this were you.

The reason you want a contract is that it makes it clear who owns what.

In some lands, if you pay someone to develop something, you own all rights in what is developed, including the IP rights, and that goes without a contract.

But in other lands, if you pay someone (who is not an employee) to create something, that other person will own the IP rights in whatever is created. You still get to use what was created—it would be pretty silly to pay a graphic designer to create a logo just for them to say you have to pay again. That's an implied license: you can use what you paid to create. You can change all that through having an agreement that says differently. And you should.

Another reason for the contract is that we now use resources from different lands, so which law do we rely upon? Best to use a contract to make it crystal clear. This should be mandatory.

Young players often try to save a few gold coins and avoid this step of forming a new contract by relying on the NDA. But NDAs are not built for long-term relationships. Plus, as you enter the next phase of the relationship, the rules change, and so you need a fresh contract.

I digress. Let's get back to protecting our golden eggs.

Let's say your big idea will be public once the big player adopts the idea. That means the NDA will restrain the big player for a while, but once your secret herbs and spices become public, the NDA won't apply to them anymore. It won't restrain the big player.

Perhaps you can file a patent application, or perhaps you can't. Maybe the idea is not patentable.

Let's look at those two options for the second phase of the relationship—remember, for the first phase, you should always start with an NDA.

Option 1 – Not Patentable

Here is where some legal magic comes into play. It all comes down to the ingredients in your contract potion and how it is mixed. This will determine if your potion results in gold raining from the skies or whether your potion explodes and turns you into a frog.

We know that the NDA won't be effective once the information becomes public, so you need a stronger legal IP potion. But what if you bound the big player to a contract potion with these ingredients:

1. I have a great big idea;
2. I'm going to let you use this big idea in the marketplace;
3. This will give you a first-mover advantage;
4. And for that first mover advantage, you will reward me handsomely by paying me a generous royalty on all your products because more people will come into your store and buy your trinkets.

Here's the difference between your simple NDA and your contract potion. In the contract, the big player isn't paying you for the confidential information. Instead, they are paying you for the benefit of the first mover advantage. This becomes material in the boxing ring because in the boxing ring, if you only had an NDA, the big player would argue that because the information is no longer confidential, even though it promised to pay you a royalty, it shouldn't have to honor that anymore because others in the village aren't similarly bound. And in some countries, that argument would win the fight.

Option 2 – Patentable (a.k.a. the Fun Stuff)

In the same scenario as above, we file our patent application and have an NDA. But we still need that second-phase contract potion with the big player.

What ingredients are in our contract potion this time?

1. I have a great big idea;
2. I'm going to let you use this big idea in the marketplace by licensing my patent to you;
3. This will give you a first-mover advantage;
4. And you will get exclusivity in the marketplace as no others can sell the same things. Customers will be enchanted into buying from you and only you;
5. For that first mover advantage and the license I have granted you, you will reward me handsomely by paying me a generous royalty on all the products

you sell because more people will come into your store and buy your trinkets.

The advantage of this option is that the big player can't try to go it alone once the idea is public because you own the patent, and they don't want to infringe the patent.

The magic continues … If you have a contract with the big player, they may terminate it. Or maybe they will breach the contract (just because some big players think they can). If they breach the contract, you can sue for damages. But if the information is public, they can keep using it—you can't stop them.

But if you have a contract with the big player whereby they license your patent, for example, if they terminate the contract, they must stop using the patent (because the contract that let them use it is now terminated). That hurts. Better still, if they breach the contract, you may be able to sue them both for breach of contract and also patent infringement. That hurts even more.

This is one of the advantages of IP rights. You can get an injunction (i.e., a stop order) against infringers using your IP rights. And that hurts them more than having to pay you money.

You see, some big players aren't honorable. They may try to get out of an agreement to cut you out of the deal. Owning and controlling the use of the IP protects you from that.

Everyone has a moral compass, but not everyone cares where it points. Protect yourself.

ProTip: Merely being a competitor is not against the law. Thus, you can't stop people competing with you. But you can stop them from breaching laws. The catch with releasing products that have new or novel features is that once those features are public, competitors may just add those features to their own product ranges. The trick to stopping them is to protect your features as much as possible (through patenting and the like).

How to Win in the Boxing Ring

So far, we've discussed how to protect your secret herbs and spices from people you speak to. But you can also protect it from strangers.

Ever wondered why people label their documents "Confidential," almost as if they are protecting nuclear launch codes? Well, that's because they are putting an innocent party on notice the information is confidential and they shouldn't use it. This becomes important in the boxing ring.

To win in the boxing ring when you are fighting over confidential information, you will have to prove some things, and your case may just hinge on whether that info is genuinely confidential. You see, it's like Colonel Sanders' eleven herbs and spices. Is it some kind of top-secret formula? Well, kind of, but not really.

In some countries, where an innocent receiver of confidential information is put on notice that the information is confidential, they have to stop use of it.

Smothering your confidential information in the word confidential signals that the information is confidential.

But a trap for young players is that they put confidential markings on material that's not confidential. When it comes to the boxing ring, the referee might not award you any points because it doesn't trust your information is confidential.

Remember that only you can protect your confidential information. This means that if your target legitimately received the information from someone else, then your rights aren't breached. I see this often with TV pitches. Producers will generally ask the pitcher to sign a document acknowledging that the producer receives pitches all day everyday and it is entirely foreseeable that the idea has been pitched before. The trouble then comes when you try to enforce your rights. How do you prove it is using your pitch rather than someone else's? This is part of the fight in the boxing ring.

A final word on confidential information. I often come across cases where a company is trying to enforce its confidential information against an ex-employee. That's great—as they should. But the trouble is they take it a bit too far and try to stop the person using their own know-how. Know-how is information that you know as part of your role that you take with you from role to role—your own bag of tricks because you are awesome at your job.

Let's use an example. Say you are a programmer and you think you have a corrupt character at the end of a line of code. But you can't work out which line has the corrupt character. Now you could painstakingly go to the end of each and every line of code and backspace to delete whatever is there … but that would take hours. So instead you Ctrl-A to select all and because everything is highlighted suddenly you can see which lines have a hidden character at the end. Knowing to do that is know-how.

Now here's the thing. A person's know-how is their own information. It can't be forgotten and no company has a right to tell you to stop using it. Imagine if you work for a company and as you leave they remind you that you have to never use all the little tricks that made you good at what you do? It doesn't make sense. But of course they can stop you using their own information. Worse, they ask you to delete all that information, but it's still stored in your brain cells. Do they expect a lobotomy?

Be careful out there dear P.I.T.C.H.ers and carefully read your employment contract in conjunction with your lawyer (still not me).

Intellectual PropertyType	Obtaining Rights	Duration of Protection	Enforcement
Copyright	Automatic upon creation. Registration (where possible)	Depends on the age of the Works. Current life of the author + 70 years.	National laws in every country which is a member of the Berne Convention.
Industrial Designs	Formal Registration Process	10 years (Australia) 15 years (United States and New Zealand) 25 years (Europe) Possible payment of an additional fee to keep registration.	National laws in the country of registration.
Patents	Formal Registration Process	20 years from the filing date (with ongoing payments of maintenance fees). Extensions of up to 5 years are possible in some cases.	National laws in the country of registration.
Trademarks	Formal Registration Process	10 years. Renewable indefinitely with active defense and use	National laws in the country of registration.
Trade Secrets	Keeping the information secret. Using non-disclosure agreements		National laws.

Wouldn't it be great if you knew what punches would be thrown in the ring *before* you walked in?

Some Common Punches in the Boxing Ring

Entitlement Disputes

Entitlement disputes are the ultimate showdowns where one person claims the throne of invention, and someone else wants a piece of the crown.

The battlefield is rife with confusion, but the main reason for this clash is the misunderstanding of what it truly means to contribute to an invention.

Picture this: An invention materializes the moment that brilliant lightbulb flickers to life in your mind. We call it "crystallization." But it doesn't occur when you simply point out a problem or say, "I need a tele-portation device." Nope, that doesn't cut it. The real invention happens when you unravel the mystery of how that teleporter works (i.e., rearranging cells through time and space to make the magic happen, a.k.a. the solution).

A patent isn't just a wish list; it's a detailed blue-print, a masterpiece that an expert in the field can use to build the invention. So, asking to be teleported isn't invention-worthy. And just because you suggested that a teleporter would be a great means of transport doesn't mean you own how the inventor solved that problem.

In the vast landscape of disputes, there's one that I frequently wade into. It's when someone identifies a problem to solve (the problem scope), and someone else crafts the solution. The problem-identifier, without more, isn't entitled to the invention. They don't wear the inventor's badge.

This tussle often unfolds in the employee-employer arena. Just because an employee stumbles upon a game-changing idea while on the company clock doesn't automatically compel him to hand the keys to the kingdom to the boss. Suppose the employee wasn't tasked with creating the solution. In most lands, the employee is the rightful owner, and the employer, usually flexing some financial muscle, is attempting a power play to claim the invention as their own. In some countries if you invent while on the company's time and using its resources, the employer does get some rights to use the invention. But it doesn't get an open slather to the invention.

CASE STUDY: Doll Wars—When Good Dolls Go to War:[9] One of the most famous entitlement disputes involves one of our favorite little dolls—the Bratz Doll. Mattel hired Carter Bryant in the "Barbies Collectable" department to design and create dolls—cool gig! While still employed by Mattel, he approached MGA with an idea for the Bratz doll. MGA jumped at the opportunity and hired Mr Bryant as a consultant. The rest of the boxing ring is a thing of legend, round after round, running for eight years, each side winning, then losing, then winning again, punch after punch. The result saw Mattel victorious.

It's a Barbie-eats-Bratz world out there. ■

It should be noted that some countries have a mandatory employee bonus when their invention enriches the employer. It's like a secret stash of compensation waiting for you, and you might not even know it exists. It's not a worldwide treasure, but if your employer has milked your invention, there might be a silver lining you've yet to discover!

Your best evidence in an entitlement dispute is your notes, drafts, drawings, emails and any other evidence of creation. Always keep your notes along

---

9   "Barbie and Bratz: The Feud Continues," n.d. https://www.wipo.int/wipo_magazine/en/2011/04/article_0006.html.

with time stamps of the material. Email yourself your notes as you go if you can't properly timestamp them. This evidence will be crucial when you need to prove who invented what or when you are accused of stealing another person's invention, or using the confidential information of your employer.

Assignment of Intellectual Property

Getting this right is what wins the fight. Intellectual property assignments are odd around the world.

In some countries, you have to put the transfer of IP (known as an assignment) in writing. In other countries, that is no problem. And in yet others, you can assign intellectual property ownership but not the right to sue for infringement.

Some assignment documents need to say certain things or be signed in a particular way. And those rules can vary based on the type of intellectual property assigned.

Imagine running a patent or trademark infringement case against an opposing party just to discover your assignment document that was downloaded from the internet was not up to snuff and you didn't own the patent or trademark. This happens in the boxing ring and it is a very expensive way to discover you should have used a lawyer to draft your documents. #truelifehurts

Documents downloaded from the internet can be cheap, until they become expensive.

Always make sure your position is intact before throwing the first punch. There was a case in Australia that involved a company undergoing restructuring. During that process it was discovered that the company had no filed trademarks. Easy peasy... just apply, right? Um no. Australia is a first-to-use country, meaning the applicant of the trademark must be the owner when the trademark is filed. The trouble came because the company using the trademark (Company A) let the company that owned Company A (known as a holding company) file for the trademark without Company A assigning the trademark to the holding company. Fast forward: what that meant was the company that sued for infringement held an invalid trademark. That stung as the issue was discovered in the boxing ring of litigation. Thus, it lost its case and had to pay the legal fees of the other party as well as its own legal fees. Ouch.

Always get an IP lawyer in the correct country to draft assignment documents. Don't download them off the web because you are sure to get what you pay for.

Forget what I just said.... Always get a qualified IP lawyer to advise you.

Joint Ownership

I've got a golden nugget of wisdom for you. When it comes to intellectual property, avoid cozying up to joint ownership. There are two kinds of countries: the ones where one co-owner can run amok without consulting the other and those where they can't. It's a proverbial "inventor marriage." In one country, you're holding hands but can let go or frolic solo with or without your partner, and in others, you're handcuffed to your "inventor spouse," going nowhere fast unless you both agree—making it possible for each co-owner to stop the invention from being used and, ultimately, resulting in sinking the invention with the weight of the ball and chain.

Don't get me wrong; I'm not telling you to become a solo act. You can still create masterpieces with your compadres, but the ownership? Keep it in the hands of a single legal entity.

Each path has its own set of perks and pitfalls. Let me regale you with a tale of another two inventors: childhood buddies who ventured into the world of invention as adults. They'd been a team for about sixty years, back when a handshake sealed the deal. It was a golden story … until it wasn't. One co-owner decided they despised their partner. The partnership crumbled, and the business slammed its doors shut. They hadn't set up a company to officially hold their intellectual property, which meant the co-owner who wanted out had the power to slam on the brakes. And they did. Sadly, the whole venture vanished overnight.

Here's another gem from Down Under. Two folks created music for a TV show. The channel wanted a musical "sting" for the show, and they approached one of the co-owners. But here's the twist: the co-owner in the spotlight went solo, recreating the musical theme without consulting the other. You can guess what happened next—a successful lawsuit for copyright infringement.

Now, hop over to the United States, where co-owners can joust for control. Picture this: Traders are racing each other to the bottom, each offering a lower price to a licensee to secure rights. I say $10, you counter with $5, and I go for $4 ... it's a never-ending spiral into the dark abyss. Nobody truly wins, and if they do, it's mere pennies compared to the value of the original treasure.

USA ProTip: In some countries (*I mean you, America, and others*), a co-owner cannot sue without the other owners joining the litigation. So what if an owner let an infringer run amok, or even pocket money from the infringer in return for not joining the court case? Would that be a clever co-owner using laws to their advantage? Or would it make them an evil sorcerer?

Here's the bottom line: your rights change from place to place. Don't think your Australian armor is invincible in the United Kingdom, and don't assume you won't need extra shields in the United States of America. Do your due diligence (confirm your rights and obligations) wherever your adventures take you. Never assume what's right in one realm holds true in another. You could wind up paying a hefty toll. Share your IP wisely, my friends.

Who should own the IP?

There is a saying of, "Those who make the money make the rules." That is certainly true. But playing fair, who should own the IP or own part of the venture?

Imagine this: One IP Wizard thinks of a problem scope and thinks he knows how to solve the problem. He invests in this project and sinks all his time and money into it. He desperately wants it to work. Just one small problem, though … he can't get it working. What does he do?

Well, he does what any self-respecting IP Wizard does. He asks his friends, who are also IP Wizards, to help out. One does and gets just as invested as our IP Wizard in getting the solution to work.

And, glorious days, it eventually does.

Our original IP Wizard is likely to try to play smart. He suddenly realizes what a great invention he has, but to pull it all off, he needs his wizard friend to continue to help out. So he promises his wizard friend a job—just a job, that's it (… nothing to see here …).

Then he starts a company, patents the invention with the company owning the invention, and makes a motsa.

But does our wizard's friend know the cards he is holding? Because our wizard and his mate are likely co-inventors and, without an agreement, they are likely to be co-owners.

This hasn't worked out well for our wizard's friend. He is a mere employee who gave up all of that time and effort for a job … just a job … that's it. And remember that our original IP Wizard's spells didn't hit the spot, he couldn't get it working without his friend.

One of two things will have happened when the company was started. Either our IP Wizard convinced his friend to assign the rights to the invention, or it wasn't assigned.

If it was assigned, it gets nasty and complicated for the friend. All is not lost but he needs to speak to his lawyer - stat!

But if it wasn't, our wizard's friend holds some cards because he may still own some of the IP, or at least he may have a right to challenge ownership (remember entitlement disputes) of the patent. He can leverage this to get a fair deal, such as a big percentage of ownership of the company that will use the intellectual property.

As to who should own the IP; one entity, but act fairly and have co-inventors fairly paid for their inventorship or own a piece of the pie.

Verify Everyone

Ever thought you were building a fortress only to discover it's a house of cards? Well, it happens, especially when you're dealing with patent matters. Contracts and promises sound great, but remember; they're only as good as the people behind them. When someone's out to steal your idea, no document will stop them. That's why you've got to be a detective in the world of intellectual property.

Let me spin a yarn about a peculiar Zoom call I once joined. The character on the screen had a certain accent, but his appearance screamed a different part of the world. Strange, right? But what confirmed my suspicions was the good old audio-video mismatch. When he spoke, his video mouth stayed shut, and when he should've been silent, his video image babbled away. In simple terms, he was playing a video of someone else. A magician's trick with a digital twist!

I wasn't about to let that slide. So, I did what any fearless IP guardian would do: I rudely interrupted and asked our mysterious actor to raise his right hand. He'd been caught red-handed (or no-handed). I knew they'd been caught, they knew they'd been caught, they knew I knew they'd been caught. But of course, he stumbled and feigned confusion. This shady character was a fraud, and his grand plan was to squeeze the essence of my client's invention out of them. Little did he know the patent was already safely in my client's name.

As if the accent-voice mishmash wasn't enough of a giveaway, here's the icing on the cake… he instantly flashed a bag of money, offering to buy shares in my client's company.

No due diligence, no questions asked, just straight to the cash. It's like offering a dragon a bag of gold; you know what it's after.

The lesson here, dear P.I.T.C.H.ers, is simple: If it seems too good to be true, it usually is. When you're dancing with deals and wheeling and dealing, make sure you've got your legal armor on. Protect your rights like you would protect a treasure chest, and don't be swayed by the glint of fool's gold.

Asset Protection Advice

Make no mistake, there are many types of fights in the boxing ring. If you want to win, you need to know the rules of asset protection first. While there are many, I've distilled it down into some basic rules (always consult a lawyer for your specific needs):

Before you file for any IP protection, you should get good legal advice on how to protect assets in your country. Imagine that you file for your patents and trademarks and other rights and jump full steam into trade. Things are going really well … until they aren't. Things start looking icy, trade has slowed, and you realize your precious company is in trouble. Eventually, the liquidators are called in because even though you tried, you just can't get out of the slump.

This is where it can go both ways. Either you lose your IP rights, or you don't.

The IP rights will be owned by the company (or some legal entity) that is using the rights (let's say that's an operating company), or they will be held in a different entity (e.g. a holding company).

If the rights are owned by the operating company (the company that is in trouble), the IP rights will be lost because the liquidators will swoop right in and sell off that asset for money to make the company pay its debts.

But what if the company that is in trouble does not own the IP rights but is licensing them? The liquidators can't take the precious IP rights, and they can start again with a new operating company. This is known as phoenixing; you rise from the ashes, born again.

Now, don't try to be too clever, dear P.I.T.C.H.ers. There is legal phoenixing and illegal phoenixing. Illegal phoenixing occurs when a company (or entity) "sells off" the IP rights (or other assets) as it is going under in an attempt to protect those rights. But liquidators have magical powers (they actually do).

Liquidators can wave their magic wand and decide that the sale never occurred. For this reason, it is best that the IP is never held in the name of the operating company, or any company or entity that it owns. But be careful here as well, P.I.T.C.H.ers—the liquidators will still try, sometimes successfully, to get their hands on the IP. Consult a qualified lawyer (and I am still not your lawyer).

A Word about the Boxing Ring

The purpose of litigation is simple—litigation resolves disputes. By filing court action, you are effectively saying to the court that you cannot resolve the dispute between the parties and you want an independent third party (a.k.a. the court) to assist and you want the decision to be binding. Think of it as a service by which a party can file an action to say, "We are in dispute and we can't decide who should win and who shouldn't. Please help." The court then acts as an independent party to decide who should win or lose. If the parties settle the matter in the meantime, that is fabulous and the court has still achieved its aim, which was to settle the dispute.

In IP matters the purpose is not to shut down the opposing party but rather to either stop them infringing your rights or to allow you to continue to trade without being harassed by the accusing party.

There are cases that should go to court and those that should not. Some cases should never see the steps of a courthouse. Simple cases where it is clear who should win or lose should not go anywhere near a court and when they do, it is generally because one party is not acting reasonably. The cases that should go to court are cases where there is genuine question over who should win or lose such as when the law is being tested.

Some Good News

What if there was such a thing as insurance for your intellectual property? Can you imagine the confidence that you would bring to the table if you had that extra protection on your side? Well, that is now available to inventors! In the IP boxing ring, you now have someone in your corner with the spit bucket, ready to put Vaseline on any cuts you sustain. Insurance provides a show of confidence in your product that was previously unavailable.

This is no longer just an analogy; this is a strategic partnership between you and your insurer. They are playing the odds and betting on your team to win. At the negotiation table, insurance can help to swing the odds in your favor and, in the case that you happen to fail, protects you financially.

This extra bit of confidence in your team and in your idea empowers you as a creator. It will give you the ability to defend your ideas with confidence, knowing that as you climb that mountain of bringing your ideas to reality, you have already clipped in with your safety line.

I've included resources at the end of the book, including links to help you find this kind of insurance. Dive into these resources and discover how you can fortify your IP rights with the added assurance of insurance. Safeguard your innovations.

IP Protection Relies on People

While the law is very black and white around IP Protection, there's one element that continues to be volatile and essential—the involvement of the right personality type.

While you might be thinking your invention is super straightforward, the people involved in the creation and protection of your IP are not. This is where the psychology of human behavior and personality types make all the difference between litigation and riches. Pay close attention to the next chapter, dear P.I.T.C.H.ers. Your success (or failure) may rely on it.

CHAPTER FOUR

WHY GREAT IDEAS DIE

(a.k.a. Test Your Type)

Personality types have a lot to do with assembling a winning start-up squad. You may be tempted to bypass this chapter, fearing it sounds too "woo," (like human design, numerology, astrology, or something along those lines), but I can tell you, it's not.

Far from it. Hundreds (nay thousands) of studies show that teams with specific personality types and temperaments succeed. And those without, never see the sunshine of success.

Think about this: Ninety percent of start-ups falter and fade within five years, not due to a lack of brilliant ideas or ambition, but due to the absence of a more elusive alchemy—the right combination of personalities.

Considering the amount of riches that hang in the balance, it only makes sense that smart founders and investors turn to highly-researched, professional personality-type tests to gauge the temperament of the people involved in any given start-up.

You can't launch a brilliant invention and sell it to the masses with a team of introverts who bury themselves in code, are scared of sales, and avoid taking risks at all costs.

There is magic in creating the right team dynamics: a blend of visionary zealots, pragmatic administrators, and the often-overlooked champions of resilience who thrive amidst chaos and uncertainty.

Modern psychology asserts that the fates of startups are irrevocably tied to the psychological makeup of their founders and early employees.

Research suggests that the ideal alchemy for a startup's success is not found in the stars but in the complementary strengths of its team members: the innovators, the executors, the strategists, and the analysts.

Even the hotheaded and impulsive have a place. That doesn't mean it is okay to throw an *I'm the main character* tantrum because having a *my-way-or-the-highway* M.O. is not playing as a team. But if you are *that* person, and those moments happen, go stand in a corner and think about how you treat people.

The corporate boardroom is the modern-day equivalent of the medieval Round Table—a table that you likely don't want to share with a mad king or a court jester. The table was round so that no one person was considered more important than another. There was an equal balance.

You want the right people at the table so that your company's future will not just be forged by the power of ideas and innovation but also by the enduring magic of human connection and collaboration.

In start-ups, a balance of strength, wisdom, and courage is essential for success. The good news? We've studied success … a *lot*. And, with the help of the psychology of success studies, we now know what blend of personalities contributes to successful start-ups.

So, how do you assess yourself and your potential start-up squad? Let's peel back the layers here to help you unearth your unique strengths and, more crucially, shine a beacon on why and when it's time to form your start-up squad.

By understanding your strengths and weaknesses, you can find the ideal collaborators whose personality types fill the gaps and make your invention journey as smooth as silk.

Assembling a Winning Start-up Squad

For a successful start-up, what personality traits do you look for in your founders, board members, and shareholders? It boils down to having a squad with at least three distinct personality types:

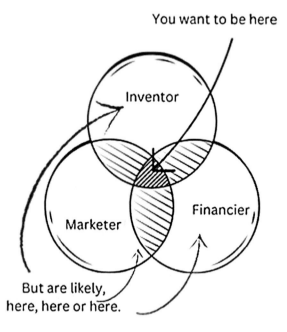

You want to be here

Inventor

Marketer

Financier

But are likely,
here, here or here.

Inventors: That's likely you. You're the brain behind the genius, the ideas person, and the origin of the IP, and your attention to detail is off the charts. But with the good comes the bad. Watch out for "inventor's syndrome," the pitfall of clutching your idea too tightly such that no one will collaborate with you because you aren't offering them a fair slice of the pie.

Marketers/Industry Insiders: They're the messengers who know the industry inside out and have all the connections. These people catapult you into the limelight and know exactly how and where to sell your idea. They are the big-picture people who take your good idea and spin it into a phenomenal buying opportunity for the masses because they magically know how the masses think.

Money: Because turning dreams into reality requires cold, hard cash. Whether it involves investing, distribution, or connections, your money maestro is the key to making it all happen. But remember, they'll want a piece of the pie (and then some).

What do all these personalities have in common? They're often fiercely independent creatures, and if your idea is going to get you rich from the P.I.T.C.H., they need to learn to play nicely together.

This is why a start-up squad is essential. One mere human rarely possesses all of the personality traits required to guide a start-up to organizational maturity and onto a successful exit path.

The examples above barely scratch the surface of the mix needed for success. So let's delve a little deeper, P.I.T.C.H.ers, and get into the research behind this modern-day crystal ball.

While the world is filled with personality tests, two have withstood the test of time and truth in testing how personalities can shape the future of a start-up:

Myers-Briggs and OCEAN. If you haven't taken these tests, no worries—you can find them both online with a simple search.

The Myers-Briggs Test

In a world of visionaries, the inventors light up the stage. Yet, even the boldest ideas need a dream team to navigate the complexities and secure that big payday.

If you're not well-acquainted with the Myers-Briggs Personality Test[10], it's like the ultimate questionnaire that sorts your personality into four key areas:

> **Energy Flow:** Are you an outgoing explorer, or do you thrive on inner contemplation?
>
> **Information Uptake:** Do you savor sensory experiences, or do you see the world as a grand puzzle?
>
> **Decision-Making Style:** Are you a logical, rational thinker, or is the human factor your North Star?
>
> **Engagement with the World:** Is your approach methodical and predictable, or do you embrace spontaneity?

These four dimensions elegantly funnel you into one of the 16 unique MBTI (Myers-Briggs) personality

---

10   Wikipedia contributors. "Myers–Briggs Type Indicator." Wikipedia, February 22, 2024. https://en.wikipedia.org/wiki/Myers%E2%80%93Briggs_Type_Indicator.

types. Understanding these types offers a window into your natural direction, focus, and choices.

If you've never delved into this treasure trove of self-discovery, go ahead and Google it—it's a real eye-opener!

For P.I.T.C.H.ers, thriving inventors typically fall under the **ENTP personality type**, which stands for:

Extroverted: They feed on external stimuli and social interactions. Shed tinkering? You bet!

Intuitive: They spot possibilities that elude the rest and whip up solutions in a jiffy.

Thinking: Logic guides their decision-making process.

Perceiving: Spontaneity is their middle name, and they keep options open like a pro.

ENTP personalities are objective thinkers, converting possibilities into full-blown ideas and plans. They're quite the rare breed, making up only 2-5 percent of the population. Entrepreneurs, to the core, are fiercely autonomous, but leadership roles and rules? Nope, not their cup of tea. Responsibility, well, they'd rather skip it. ENTPs are opportunistic thinkers, often connecting the unconnectable—perfect inventor material!

But like all good stories, there's a twist: ENTP's strengths can also be their Achilles' heel in the business management arena. They're the first to jump ship when things get tough, with a head full of ideas that rarely get realized.

Here's the silver lining: ENTPs are a rare breed. This rarity means that to achieve profound success, the average ENTP should partner with others, especially those with marketing or money-making personality traits.

Inventors obsess over the finer details but might miss the bigger picture. Marketers, on the other hand, see the grand scheme but don't sweat the small stuff. These two personality types rarely unite in a single person (2-5 percent are ENTPs).

How does Myers-Briggs relate to innovation?

Damian Killen and Gareth Williams' insightful book "Type and Innovation" delves into four innovation phases: Discover, Decide, Define, and Deliver.[11]

Your personality type is pivotal in determining where your innovation shines brightest. Specifically, it hinges on P.I.T.C.H.ers' preference within the Sensing v Intuition spectrum (S/N), dictating how they gather

---

11   https://www.amazon.com/INTRODUCTION-TYPE-INNOVA-TION-DAMIAN-KILLEN/dp/B00F102VPQ

information, and Judging v Perceiving (J/P), which reveals how they engage with the external world.

Here's the scoop on which Myers-Briggs types thrive in each of these innovative phases:

Discover: This is the realm of generating myriad ideas. The NP crowd excels here, driven by curiosity to churn out fresh concepts.

Decide: Where the best ideas take center stage. The NJ crowd thrives, craftily strategizing to bring these ideas to life.

Define: The stage of simplification and refinement. The SP types love this part, employing trial and error to perfect the process before execution.

Deliver: This is where efficient execution reigns supreme. The SJ crowd shines, focusing on streamlining, enhancing, and optimizing processes.

The OCEAN Test

The OCEAN test spells out the Big Five personality traits, also known as the Five Factor Model (FFM), a widely accepted model in psychological research.[12]

The five traits are Openness, Conscientiousness,

---

12   Jenniferd. "The Big 5 Personality Traits in the Workplace." Michigan State University, July 12, 2023. https://www.michiganstateuniversityonline.com/resources/leadership/lead-your-team-with-big-five-model/.

Extraversion, Agreeableness, and Neuroticism, often remembered by the acronym OCEAN.

Openness

Conscientiousness

Extraversion

Agreeableness

Neuroticism

Each person has each of these traits, but people fit on a scale of low to high—where they fall on the scale[13] is the question.

Openness (to Experience): Characterized by a strong intellectual curiosity, creativity, a preference for novelty, and a variety of experiences.

People with high openness are imaginative, curious, experimental, are abstract thinkers, and embrace challenges.[13]

People with low openness are practical and conventional, they have a narrow interest range, and they do not embrace change.[13]

---

13   Jenniferd.

Meet Alex, an avid reader and amateur painter who thrives on trying new things. Whether exploring ancient ruins in Greece or learning a new musical instrument, Alex's love for diverse experiences makes every day an adventure.

Conscientiousness: Associated with being disciplined, well-organized, punctual, and dependable. Conscientious individuals tend to show self-discipline, act dutifully, and aim for achievement.

People with high conscientiousness are disciplined, detail-oriented, dutiful, organized, and reliable.[14] (*I am clear evidence that people can fall strongly into this category despite the state of their desk…*)

People with low conscientiousness are spontaneous, flexible, negligent, unreliable, and procrastinate.[14]

---

14   Jenniferd.

Meet Nic, who meticulously plans each day with a to-do list. Known among her friends as the one who never flakes, Nic balances a full-time job, volunteers on weekends, has recently taken to writing books, and never misses a brisk daily walk. Nic dreams of being a superhero.

Extraversion: Reflects a person's inclination to seek stimulation in the company of others, as well as the energy and positive emotions that people tend to experience in a social environment.

People with high extraversion are social, enthusiastic, assertive, opinionated, and adventurous.[15]

People with low extraversion are introverted, passive, reserved, quiet, and self-sufficient.[15]

Meet Charlie, who is the life of the party—never shy to meet new people or start a conversation. With an extensive social circle, Charlie loves big gatherings and often feels energized after spending time with friends.

Agreeableness: This trait features attributes such

---

15   Jenniferd

as trust, altruism, kindness, affection, and other pro-social behaviors.

People with high agreeableness are empathetic, cooperative, trustworthy, good-natured, and straightforward.[16]

People with low agreeableness are independent, uncooperative, overly critical, dominant, and agonistic.[16]

Meet Sam. Sam is the one everyone turns to for support. Always ready to lend an ear or a helping hand, Sam's empathetic nature and readiness to trust makes for a reliable and compassionate friend.

Neuroticism: Individuals with high levels of neuroticism experience emotional instability, anxiety, moodiness, irritability, and sadness.

People with high neuroticism are unstable, anxious, irritable, self-conscious, and are worriers.[16]

People with low neuroticism are composed, calm, even-tempered, resilient, and confident.[16]

---

16   Jenniferd.

Meet Riley, who often finds himself worrying about the future, dwelling on past mistakes, and getting upset by small inconveniences. Despite being successful, Riley's high-strung nature makes it hard to enjoy achievements or relax without feeling anxious. Poor Riley. Riley may sound sad, but we still need Riley.

Now that we have the personality traits down, let's look at the maturity level of companies.

The Six Stages of Company Maturity

Much like the stages of human development, companies undergo distinct phases of maturity and growth. Understanding these growth stages is akin to possessing the key to unlocking the ideal personality types crucial for success at each juncture.

Let's unravel the intricacies of the six stages together, shall we?

1. Discovery:

During this initial phase, start-ups concentrate on validating whether they address a significant problem (that's chapter two) and if there's potential interest in their solution. Key events include the formation of the founding team, extensive customer interviews, identification of the value proposition, development of minimally viable products, enrollment in an accelerator or incubator, the friends and family financing round, and the onboarding of first mentors and advisors.

This phase is about exploring new ideas, validating concepts, and being open to various possibilities and solutions. Openness to experience is crucial here, as it involves creativity, intellectual curiosity, and a willingness to explore uncharted territories.

2. Validation

In the validation stage, start-ups aim to secure early confirmation that people are genuinely interested in their product, demonstrated through financial transactions or attention. Events include the refinement of core features, attainment of first paying customers, initial user growth, implementation of metrics and analytics, seed funding, critical hires, potential pivots, and achieving product-market fit.

As start-ups move to validate their products and services, conscientiousness becomes key. This stage requires discipline, organization, and a focus on achieving set goals—traits that conscientious individuals excel in.

3. Efficiency

Efficiency becomes the focal point as start-ups fine-tune their business model and enhance the effectiveness of their customer acquisition process. The goal is to acquire customers efficiently, avoiding the pitfalls of scaling with a leaky bucket. Events during this stage involve refining the value proposition, overhauling user experience, optimizing the conversion funnel, achieving viral growth, and identifying repeatable sales processes or scalable customer acquisition channels.

In the efficiency stage, the focus is on refining and optimizing processes. Team members high on the agreeableness scale—with its emphasis on cooperation, trust, and empathy—are beneficial for team collaboration and customer relationship management, which are crucial for improving efficiency.

4. Scale

With the scale stage, start-ups hit the accelerator, pushing aggressively for growth. Key events include significant A-Round investment funding, substantial customer acquisition efforts, enhancements in back-end scalability, initial executive hires, process implementation, and the establishment of departments.

Scaling a business requires extensive networking, negotiations, and relationship building. Extraversion, with its inclination towards social interaction and high energy, is advantageous in this high-stakes, outward-facing stage.

5 & 6. Profit Maximization and Renewal or Decline

In the profit maximization phase, a company focuses on increasing its profits to the highest possible level. This stage typically occurs after the business has established a solid market presence and achieved a sustainable rate of growth.

If a company fails to effectively refresh itself, it may enter a decline phase. During this stage, the company experiences diminishing relevance and financial performance.

The refresh or decline phase demands strategic foresight, adaptability, and sometimes tough decision-making. Companies that successfully navigate this phase can emerge stronger and more competitive, while those that fail to adapt may face an irreversible decline.

In these phases, where strategic decisions about the future of the company are made amidst potential stress and uncertainty, a certain level of neuroticism might be beneficial. It can lead to caution and risk-awareness, helping to navigate the company through challenging times.

Now that we have personality traits and phases of the maturity of a company properly defined, how do the personality traits fit into the start-up phases?

Company Maturity	Beneficial Personality Trait	Negative Personality Trait
Discovery	Openness (creative, curious)	Neuroticism (uncertainty, stress)
Validation	Conscientiousness (diligent, methodical), Agreeableness (responsive to feedback)	Neuroticism (anxiety about viability), Openness (over-fixation on original idea)
Efficiency	Conscientiousness (organized, efficient), Agreeableness (team-oriented)	Neuroticism (stress under optimization pressures), Openness (resistance to procedural change)
Scale	Extraversion (expansive, energetic), Openness (adaptable, growth-oriented)	Neuroticism (risk of overexpansion), Conscientiousness (potential inflexibility in processes)
Profit Maximization	Neuroticism(caution and risk awareness), Agreeableness (maintaining relationships),	Openness (resistance to innovation), Agreeableness (overemphasis on current relationships at the expense of new opportunities)
Decline	Neuroticism(caution and risk awareness), Agreeableness (maintaining relationships), Extraversion (efforts to re-engage market)	Conscientiousness (rigidity, resistance to necessary changes)

For the very luckiest of you, some steps will be a breeze, while others will be a beast. This is why, if you are launching a start-up, you need to partner with people whose strengths makeup for your weaknesses.

Find Your Inventor's Ikigai

Ever heard of 'Ikigai'? It's a Japanese concept, the place where your passion, mission, vocation, and profession intersect. Find it, and you've found your unique purpose, paving the road to profound success and fulfillment. To discover your Ikigai, ask yourself: What do I adore? What am I a virtuoso at? What does the world crave? What can I rake in the dough from?

Applying this, you can align your choices with your core values and aspirations. Monetizing your ideas follows a similar path. You need to pinpoint your skills, identify what the world demands, determine what pays the bills, and zero in on what sets your soul on fire.

Sharing the Sauce

Once people work out that you have something special, everyone is going to want in! You've got the secret sauce, and everyone wants it. There are those who deserve a piece of the action and those who don't. You'll have everyone coming out of the shadows trying to claim a piece and convince you they are your newest bestie. Congratulations, you likely have 100 new besties, including your uncle's brother's goldfish's siblings.

The trick, dear P.I.T.C.H.ers, is to work out who deserves a piece of your start-up and who is just trying to ride on your coattails. This is where you need to play the smart game. Play it smart and fair, because you need your start-up squad just as much as they need you.

So Who Should Get Ownership?

In the world of inventors, there's more than one way to contribute to an invention. There's defining the problem scope and the solution of course, but there's also the person (or people) who materially contribute as part of your start-up squad and who deserve ownership in the final result of the start-up. These are the people who are a pivotal part of your start-up squad and who are set to continue with the start-up on an ongoing basis.

Then there are supporting players who might provide services only once or once in a while. Think of these players as an ensemble of nobles, advisors, and entertainers in your medieval court—not the main characters, just those who play a supporting role from time to time.

So who should get a slice of your start-up? Who deserves to have Lord or Lady status and be given a parcel of land in exchange for supporting the King?

Founders need to have a balanced approach to who gets a share of ownership. They shouldn't give away too much too early, but they should also not have inventor's syndrome; a term to describe inventors who think they are the "main character" and who refuse to give up a reasonable share of ownership to those who genuinely deserve it. Inventors need to recognize that whilst they have contributed the solution to the problem scope, the others in the start-up squad have also contributed their skills, time, and energy. Inventors need to respect the contributions of those players; some of them identified the problem scope allowing the invention in the first place.

The term "sweat equity" is a term used to refer to equity (i.e., ownership) in a company (or something) paid for by the sweat of the brow. Members of your start-up squad may contribute sweat equity but sometimes also finances. Or they may contribute their networking skills, the invention itself, etc. The trick here is not to provide ownership to those who only provide sweat on a temporary basis.

How you configure your start-up is entirely up to you and should only be decided in conjunction with your lawyer—still not me—and your accountant—again, still not me. But expect that a person who is pivotal to the ongoing success of the start-up, is working on an ongoing basis, and has been with the company from the start would rightly feel that they should have some ownership of the venture. You founded the company together. These players may not sit at the board table, but that doesn't mean they shouldn't be awarded shares for their contribution.

Imagine this: A business partner you respect materially contributes to your start-up through their massive network, they help you hone the solution/invention and suggest different things. They make all the right introductions, are great with contracts, and are putting in the hours to build the dream. They have done all of this work without pay because they think they are part of the start-up squad. Then the fated day arrives, the company is formed, and it's go go go. But then they discover, to their horror, they are offered an employee agreement and expected to assign all of the IP they just created to the start-up for no contribution or just the contribution of being able to buy shares later. They would be insulted.

ProTip: Don't insult your colleagues.

Contrast that to founders who are transparent with their start-up squad and have an agreement that sets down the ground rules moving forward. Everyone knows what is expected, knows what they contribute, and knows what they can expect by way of ownership.

Founders need a shareholder agreement (if they are

running a company) or some other shareholder-type contract. This is an agreement that sets the ground rules for the running of the company, which binds both the company and the shareholders. The importance of this agreement cannot be stressed enough. Shareholder agreements are the unsung heroes of business harmony. They set down what happens if someone wants out, if someone wants in, what kind of decisions can be made by the board of directors, and what decisions must be made by the owners. Importantly, it sets down what is considered a successful exit and whether the owners can be forced to sell.

Imagine this: A big buyer comes along and desperately wants in! Happy days, but what if the big buyer wants all the ownership and one owner doesn't want to sell? Well, then, the shareholder agreement comes into play and determines what should happen.

But there is a negative to giving away too much ownership too soon. Imagine a start-up that gives away too much to a mere supporting player. A founder was in a money crunch when he was launching his start-up but wanted a logo, so he gave away 5 percent of his company for a logo which was promptly replaced a year or so later. The issue came ten years later, after the founder had toiled away, building his business and battling against competitors, when he finally saw a light in the form of an offer to buy the whole company. But he couldn't find the person who had created the logo to get the paperwork signed—that person still owned 5 percent of the company even though all he did was create a (now abandoned) logo back in the day. The founder had given away part of the ownership for a short-term gain. When you need material created by supporting players, consider whether you really should give away ownership or you can compensate the person with money instead.

There's another lesson from this story. He was tight for funds when starting up, so he avoided having a shareholder agreement. If he had that shareholder agreement, he would have been able to sell the whole company to the buyer by signing on behalf of the missing shareholder. The whole deal was held up looking for the missing shareholders.

ProTip: Shareholdership is a bit like a marriage. You shouldn't enter into one until you are sure that you know who your fellow shareholders are. You don't necessarily have to be soulmates, but you need to know that you can trust and work with fellow shareholders. It can be challenging to work alongside individuals with intense and/or dominant personality traits. Assertive and charismatic personalities may use their personalities to control and manipulate situations, ultimately affecting the bottom line. If other shareholders excel at hiding their true intentions, you may not notice things have gone off the rails until it's too late to do anything about it. Those who are being manipulated are often the last ones to realize they're the victim. Like any marriage, personality conflicts, a difference in long-term vision, deceit, or manipulation can easily ruin the shareholdership. Unique and different personalities are acceptable. Abuse is not. Long story short, before committing to a shareholder agreement, take the time to understand and assess the character and intentions of those you're going into business with. This can save you from potential conflicts and issues that might arise from partnering with someone whose goals and methods don't align with yours.

Get a shareholder agreement and know your fellow shareholders and directors—you will thank me later.

Ask yourself if the person is staying as part of the team and will continue with the start-up. If yes, do they contribute enough for ownership, or are they a mere employee? If they aren't a permanent fixture, consider paying in money.

Supporting Player Personalities

Your cast of team members, don't always need to be part of the start-up squad. You can have supporting players that provide a hand from time to time. Let's go through a few you might need.

Lawyer

Dear P.I.T.C.H.ers, you knew this was coming. But your lawyer is your right hand when founding a company. They can help you with all the contracts you need, like NDAs, customer agreements, shareholders agreements, asset protection advice, and of course, all the investment documents you will need. They can guide you on what IP needs to be protected and what can be protected. They will be your knight in shining armor in the boxing ring. Don't dismiss how important it is to have a lawyer in your corner.

Patent Agent

These are the people who will draft your patent and, hopefully, push it through to grant.

Be warned, P.I.T.C.H.ers—not all patent agents are created equally. They each have their own specialty. Don't go to a "life science" (i.e., pharmaceutical) patent agent to have them draft a patent about a new mechanical engine.

The trick here is to find a patent agent that specializes in your kind of invention and make sure they understand it. If they don't understand it, they won't be able to draft it properly.

Do not be tempted to do this yourself, P.I.T.C.H.ers. This is a highly specialized skill, and if you mess it up, it could cost you millions, and your patent may well be invalid.

If you need to find a patent agent, check out our resources section at the end of this book.

* * *

We've discussed OCEANS above, and there are a myriad of free online tests available to assess yourself. Just search for one online.

There are also organizations that will conduct similar testing for your team. This is helpful as they show how teams interact and allow you to assess and build your team with the personality type in mind. These tests allow you to determine what personality type you may be missing and target that type for your new hire.

In short, P.I.T.C.H.ers, I am saying, don't try to do this alone unless your exit strategy is to get out quickly. I discuss what exit strategy favors what personality type in the next chapter.

So, P.I.T.C.H.ers, time to embrace your personality type and let it steer you to innovation greatness. The kind of business model you choose and the team you create to support your invention will be the foundations of your success ... or failure.

CHAPTER FIVE

MIND THE SHARP CURVES
(a.k.a. Chart Your Exit)

B ehind every groundbreaking idea is an inventor who looks at the world in a way no one else has before. It takes a kaleidoscope of strengths, ambitions, and quirks to bring our ideas to life, likely because the road to idea realization is no straight highway. It's more akin to a route through the mountains—winding roads, sharp curves, and cliffs off to one side.

CASE STUDY: Consider Thomas Edison. At one point, 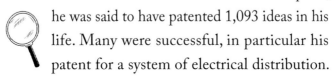 he was said to have patented 1,093 ideas in his life. Many were successful, in particular his patent for a system of electrical distribution. There was also the long-burning incandescent light bulb, of course. Edison didn't actually invent the light bulb but modified it to work more practically, then proceeded to repeatedly have his photo taken in front of it, making the lightbulb synonymous with the Edison name. He invented the dictaphone, the alkaline battery, the phonograph, and many modern appliances and devices found in homes across the world. So what does this all mean about his ability to invent successfully?

Let's start with the math. If you patent over one thousand ideas, you're bound to see your fair share of failure. And Edison did.

Edison may have founded hundreds of successful companies and, at the same time, lost several fortunes to inventions gone awry. Some fun examples are pianos and furniture made out of cement, electric pens, a very creepy talking doll, and ink for the blind.

So what type of personality does it take to work—according to some biographies—fifty hours straight at a time to essentially change the world? Would he have passed today's personality tests in terms of being a successful inventor, destined for riches?

Some historians say Edison had horrid business sense, was absent-minded, and had a strange eating disorder. But there is no doubt that he was a genius. He had a gift for sharing his ideas with the press and the world at large (essentially generating his own hype).

Building on the previous Test Your Type chapter, you see evidence of Edison in at least two of the three Venn diagram circles—inventor (most definitely), marketer (he was always in the spotlight), money (less so, but his marketing skills helped draw investors). He also had the lion's share of the ENTP personality (extroverted, intuitive, thinking, and perceiving) that fit inventors who thrive and succeed.

If you were to try to find which personality types the Myers-Briggs test would have funneled Edison into, it was surely the lion's share of the ENTP personality type (that's *extroverted*, *intuitive*, *thinking*, and *perceiving*, to recap).

Edison is described by many as being *extroverted*; he fed on external stimuli and social interactions. He was known for his mastery of showmanship with the press and the world at large. Shed tinkering? Absolutely. Especially if one's shed grew to the size of a 25' by 100' "invention factory" on thirty-four acres of land (Menlo Park). He was *intuitive*, spotting possibilities and solutions faster than others. He was a *thinking* personality type; using logic to guide his decision-making process (though this area was surely influenced by investors, board members, and managers). And above all, he fit the *perceiving* personality description in that spontaneity was his middle name. How else could he have made so many inventions in a single lifetime? So many ideas in a single day.

He was able to thrive in each innovation phase (discover, decide, define, deliver). If we look at the

OCEAN Test and the many biographies written on Edison (including the multitudes of invention and engineering notes he left behind when he died), he was likely high O (openness to experience), low C (conscientiousness), high E (extraversion), low A (agreeable), and mid-to-high N (neuroticism).

All this to say, he wasn't everything to everyone. He was lacking in key areas, which required that he have a team to help support his ideas and bring them to life. Where he fell short, his start-up squads and company teams must have filled in the gaps. Edison's companies employed thousands of engineers, scientists, and investors. He had the right investors and managers to pick up where he left off, bringing his ideas to life and changing the lives of everyone his work touched. ∎

The lesson here is even some of the most successful amongst us need a mix of personalities. Don't hire someone with your personality type, hire someone who compliments you and fills the spots you miss. Don't hire someone who is great at their job just to tell them what to do. First, it is disrespectful but also futile. Intelligent people will soon become bored with being micromanaged and will walk.

Now that we've put type tests into perspective, we need to get back on the road toward taking your idea to the next level. Buckle up! This might get a little bit intense.

Money v Not So Much: Choosing the Right Business Model

P.I.T.C.H.ers, if I had a dollar for every inventor who came to me with dreams of "commercializing" their ingenious creations, I would be Bezos-caliber-rich.

What they're really gunning for is to birth a company that churns out profits thanks to their inventive brainchildren. Don't get me wrong; it's a well-trodden path, littered with the promise of gold coins and endless riches, despite the fact that it should likely have a "Wrong Way" or "Do Not Enter" sign posted for most who travel there. Yet, it's far from the only road to Money Town. Some folks might as well don a "Wrong Way" sign for this journey if their personalities and skills don't play nicely with this brand of monetization.

You have learned the personality traits of successful start-ups. You need a squad; some people are just not cut out for squads, so they chart a different exit.

In the realm of inventing for profit, there are three routes you can take:

1. Invent to Sell
2. Invent to License

3. Invent to Commercialize

Let's evaluate each one together, starting with the one *Shark Tank* aficionados love most because they believe it's the holy grail of profiting from your ideas. This one requires a lot of armor along the way.

Invent to Sell (a.k.a. Take the Money and Run)

Your lightbulb moment strikes, and you create something sure to be your golden ticket to a treasure trove of cash. You craft your invention and then hand it over to another trader, waving goodbye to your rights in the process. This can either be a one-time sale or an upfront fee with potential royalties down the line.

This path reduces the risk of trusting the wrong company with your invention. They might opt just to put it on the shelf and let it gather dust, instead of helping it change the world or generate riches. But when you sell for a flat up front fee, that's okay—they are only hurting themselves. So if you are selling for an upfront one-time fee, shelved inventions may not concern you, but if you are banking on receiving royalties later, you will want to ensure your invention is being sold to an honorable company.

Going the invention-to-sell route runs the risk of

seller's remorse. For example: you sell to a buyer for a handsome profit, but as you're counting your money, said buyer succeeds beyond your wildest dreams with "your" invention. You're left wishing you hadn't given up your rights so easily. This is a scenario to watch for because it happens often. Many buyers may have an interest in convincing you they aren't going to make much profit with your idea. This allows them to propose a lower purchase price.

Many inventors who would rather steer clear of the business world and minimize risk-taking like this pathway because it ultimately offers the opportunity to take their money and run! Think of them as professional inventors. But here's the kicker: this approach is no walk in the park. Patience is the name of the game while you wait for the payout.

The Winning Route:

- Invent your heart out.
- Secure patents globally and speed up the patent approval process in key countries.
- Once your patents are locked and loaded, approach companies in your industry and pitch your invention. Your bargaining chip? Those hard-earned rights.

CASE STUDY: This technique can be extremely effective. There is a prolific inventor who makes small toy-like things that are impossibly cheap and irresistible. He knows how to play the patent game P.I.T.C.H.ers. He has no head for business, is a loner, and just loves inventing.

So he *invents to sell* his patents/ideas, etc.

But he plays a long game. He first files a patent in his local country, then around the world securing patent rights. This takes at least three years. He then approaches organizations that love to sell small gadgets to parents to appease screaming children in shopping centers. And he hits paydirt every single time. Last I heard he sells his patent portfolio for a cool $50 million a pop. Then he does it again and again. But he is not alone; this is a common story. ■

Ideal Personalities

Each of the three distinct pathways for monetizing your inventions aligns with particular personality traits and characteristics. Those who gravitate toward inventing to sell typically embody the following personality types:

Decisive Dynamos: Entrepreneurs embarking on the journey to sell their inventions are often known for their decisiveness. These knights (no gender intended) thrive in making rapid, well-considered decisions that expedite their projects and open doors to the next big thing. They don't want to get involved in business; they just want to cash in and get out quickly.

Objective-Oriented Visionaries: For these individuals, the ultimate goal of monetizing their invention quickly holds paramount importance. Their focus is laser-sharp on the destination, prioritizing the achievement of financial success over the intricate and drawn-out process of building and scaling a business around their innovation.

Risk Minimizers: Selling an invention tends to appeal to those who want a low-risk option. They are inclined to jump at the chance to cash in on their innovative idea as early as possible, rather than diving headfirst into the time-consuming and resource-intensive long game of building a full-fledged business entity.

This exit strategy also suits those who invent outside their industry or inside well-established industries. They don't need to know the industry to cash in, they just need the connections to open doors. *And, of course, they need a good sales pitch.* They also can sell to well-established businesses that have their supply and sale channels well established.

In the realm of invention, these personalities are the driving forces behind expedited success. For them, the ultimate prize is the transformation of their innovative ideas into fast financial rewards.

Scams v Protection (a.k.a. Winning by Staying Out of the Boxing Ring)

Some industrious buyers will attempt to rob you of your rewards.

The beauty of the invent-to-sell model is that the risk of success of the product lies with the buyer. Some buyers will try to share that risk.

What they will say is:

- Why don't you sell it to me for a smaller price;
- In return, I will reward you with a cut of the action.

Think of how many times you've seen this exact scenario play out on one of the invention-pitching television shows. There's a reason for that. A good investor is going to get as much value for as little risk and expense as they can. It's not personal, it's just business, right?

Think of the lessons from our prior chapters. Let's say you are convinced to sell your patent to a company but you also want ongoing royalties from sales of products: What happens if the company does not perform? Worse, what happens if they sell the patent to someone else? Or if they simply decide they don't want to be bound to the contract at all? If they own the IP you can't sue them for IP infringement. All you can do is sue for contract breach and that is not ideal. Even worse, what if the company gets into trouble and shuts down? You receive nothing and you lose the IP rights.

Careful here dear P.I.T.C.H.ers, this technique requires a lot of due diligence on the buyer.

The lesson here is that if you are going to enter into a deal where you sell the patent but also put your hand out for royalties, you need to be able to trust the company you're selling to and put clauses into your contract that protect you.

Always Use Protection

Shield your invention before you go knocking on corporate doors. Here's why: you will likely need to sign an NDA (non-disclosure agreement), yours or theirs (you may hear of both sides having NDAs, but not often, as they would likely clash with each other).

NDAs are like guardians of confidential information. As long as your invention remains under wraps and the people you're talking to follow the rules, you're good. However, there's a dark side to this story. Not everyone plays by the rules. Your invention might not remain hush-hush, or someone else might have already pitched a similar idea to these corporate bigwigs—or worse; the corporate bigwigs think they are bigger than a mere agreement.

When you lay an idea on the table, the folks across from you immediately start dissecting it with the mission of finding out if they can snag it without you.

Some will respect the NDA and others? Not so much. So, you need to give them a darn good reason to choose you and your invention. Exclusivity tends to be the magic word, and patents hand it to them on a silver platter.

Your presence in the market might sweeten the deal, too. They might just want your invention as a shortcut to launching their own product, meaning that if you don't guard your rights, they could very well swoop in and steal your idea and any potential to make money from it. In short: get your patents in first so the bigwigs can't run off with your invention.

The invent-to-sell approach can be a winner, but remember, not every buyer is looking for the same thing. Each buyer has their own appetite for risk. Some are daredevils who aren't afraid to take the plunge into the unknown by betting on the unsold, the uncommercialized, or the "Is this even going to sell?" product.

And others? They're all about safety. They want a sure thing that'll start raking in the dollars—pronto!

Non-risk takers won't usually give up their gold until later in the game; they will play it safe, only buying into well-proven ideas.

Invent to Licence (a.k.a. Piña Colada on the Beach)

Contrary to the invent-to-sell exit strategy we just explored, another potent avenue involves licensing your rights to a company. Much like the invent-to-sell approach, this strategy finds its sweet spot in well-established industries, providing a nuanced approach to commercial success.

We've all been captivated by the allure of *Shark Tank*-style shows where passionate entrepreneurs showcase ideas they hope will be considered groundbreaking to a panel of investors who can love them or leave them. Most of the entrepreneurs in this show are fueled by the desire to enter the market independently.

However, this path isn't always the most pragmatic route to success.

Firstly, many aspiring inventors seek entry into saturated markets, perhaps inventing a product such as hole-proof socks. The socks market is a fiercely competitive landscape ruled by a few long-running companies that design, manufacture, license, and distribute socks. Numerous sock manufacturers already tout "hole-proof" claims, producing at lower costs and boasting established sales channels. Initiating a new sock company under these circumstances might feel like (or actually be) a futile endeavor.

Secondly, overlooking intellectual property protection can lead to costly repercussions. Competitors can swiftly replicate your concept once your innovative socks hit the market, leaving you sidelined. However, having robust protection opens the door to licensing opportunities, offering a way to monetize your idea without risking it all.

Hole-proof socks are a good example of why you will want to be strategic about how you handle your invention.

The invent-to-license approach is flexible and lets you maximize your potential to succeed *and* get creative in how you do so. You can even combine it with other exit strategies for additional income streams or a substantial windfall. Those beachside piña coladas won't fund themselves, P.I.T.C.H.ers!

Picture this: You invent a groundbreaking tool for installing roof tiles. You create a unique licensing opportunity by obtaining a patent for both the tool and the installation method. As you use the tool in your local area, you license the method to others when selling them the tool, generating additional income effortlessly.

But it doesn't stop there. You can diversify your licensing approach, catering to different market segments. License the right to install existing structures to one party, new big structures to another, and new small structures to yet another, spreading risk and boosting income. It's brilliant.

And the beauty? Money keeps flowing in. Expand your horizons by protecting your invention overseas, potentially repeating the entire licensing process abroad. You can simplify the process by licensing to a main distributor per country, allowing them to sublicense to others while handling enforcement, revenue collection, and administrative tasks.

Imagine if, instead of a roofing tool, you invented a medical device that could be used in procedures for both humans and animals. You could increase your revenue by licensing it to both veterinary and human health separately.

While not strictly an exit, the invent-to-license technique is as effective as a full exit.

Imagine desiring a hands-off approach, simply wanting to bask on a beach with a piña colada. Licensing your rights exclusively to an existing industry giant allows you to deal with just one organization, leaving them to run with the product. At the same time, you enjoy a steady stream of rewards. Cheers to a licensing strategy that lets you sip on success without the hassle!

Scams v Protection (a.k.a. Winning in the Boxing Ring)

Making a successful exit is not always as graceful as a blissful beach retreat with piña coladas. Sometimes, it feels like sand in your hair and a second-degree sunburn. Watchfulness is your ally in this realm of opportunity. Being wary of cunning con artists and shrewd negotiators is your shield. Each player in this game is a professional, taking their role seriously. It's unlikely for this to be anyone's first time in the ring.

The biggest challenge lies in distinguishing between the con artist and the legitimate business dealmaker. It's a task that, unfortunately, doesn't come with a foolproof manual. However, armed with vigilance and the guidance of a savvy lawyer (remember; I'm not your lawyer), you have a much better chance of navigating the tricky waters.

To succeed at the invent-to-license pathway, you'll want to study those who have stepped into the ring before you. Learn from the (often bitter) experiences of others by taking a front-row seat at the boxing ring. Watch what punches are thrown, learn how to anticipate the blows, and get ready for your turn in the ring—because it *will* come.

Ideal Personalities for the Invent-to-License Pathway

Collaborative: Opting for a licensing approach entails creating a collaborative partnership with another company. Entrepreneurs who thrive on collaboration, value partnerships, and excel at working closely with others are naturally inclined toward this method.

Skillful Negotiators: Licensing agreements necessitate the art of negotiation. Those with strong negotiation skills who can secure favorable terms and royalties with partner companies are best suited for this model.

Flexibility-Oriented: Entrepreneurs who lean towards licensing their inventions tend to be more flexible in their approach. They are willing to grant another company the right to utilize and commercialize their invention, all in exchange for royalties. This flexibility reflects a mindset that may not be too concerned with maintaining strict control over their product or technology, just as long as those royalty checks keep coming in.

Anti-Business: Entrepreneurs with no interest in business and don't want to be hassled by running a business will prefer the invent-to-license method. The ability to exclusively license your invention allows you to step out of the business game and still make money as if you were in the thick of it all.

Protection

The invent-to-license pathway can be a goldmine, but before you strike it rich, you'll have to watch for scammers, thieves, copycats, slackers, and infringers. Here's how to start:

- Shield yourself with license agreements and the right lawyer. Understanding the intricacies of license agreements will become paramount, which is where your lawyer—a good one, preferably—becomes your invaluable ally, your protector. Their job is to make sure you're not caught in a legal quagmire.

- Royalties, the sweet yield from your intellectual property, necessitate a keen eye on your piece of the pie to make sure you get as much as you're owed, at the frequency in which you are owed it. The ability to audit the use of your invention is vital. Craft this clause meticulously so that you have the power to examine the books of the licensee thoroughly. By beginning regular audits from the outset; you set the tone and deter any shady maneuvers. Proactive auditing prevents awkward situations where suspicion prompts a sudden audit, potentially insulting the licensee.

- Choosing between exclusive and non-exclusive licensing requires careful consideration. Exclusive licenses may limit your ability to exploit your invention. A nuanced approach splits license-granting exclusivity for specific industries, areas, or sales channels. Non-exclusive licensing may be the right answer at the time, but what if another big player wants an exclusive relationship? Whether the relationship is exclusive or nonexclusive also determines who can sue for infringement. Get legal advice on your local laws to see what rules you can put down for licensing and what rules you can't.

- Performance indicators (or KPIs) and termination clauses are your tools for ensuring the licensee upholds their end of the bargain.

Without these, you risk being stuck with a non-performing licensee, especially concerning exclusive licenses.

- Beware of competitors posing as licensees with nefarious intentions. Craft termination clauses that protect your interests, allowing you the flexibility to react if the licensee doesn't perform or appears to be engaging in questionable activities.

- Termination of exclusive license agreements can be challenging. Strike a balance that protects your interests without unduly burdening the licensee.

- Deciding who has the right to sue for infringement is a crucial consideration. Exclusive licensees might be best suited for this role, but be aware of the legal nuances in different jurisdictions. Sometimes an owner can't sue unless the exclusive licensee is also a party to the court case and vice versa.

- For non-exclusive license agreements, termination should also be on your radar, especially when another distributor shows promise and seeks exclusivity.

- Ownership of trademarks is a strategic move. Retain control over the trademark to safeguard your brand even after parting ways with the licensee.

- Protect yourself against copycats and distributors supplementing their stock with unauthorized copies by applying secret markings or "fingerprints" to your products. This can be in the form of a design feature only you know about or, in the case of published Work, might be something such as purposely added misinformation (careful here). These measures provide added security so that when an opposing party steals your IP-protected Work, you have only to point to the numerous secret markings or misinformation to show the Work has been stolen.

- Social media pages and other assets should revert to you post-termination. Keep an eye on ownership details to avoid complications.

Stay vigilant, be savvy, and let your lawyer guide this intricate dance of intellectual property and licensing.

> **ProTip:** When negotiating, be cautious of those suggesting you use the same lawyer. Never trust a person insisting, "Just use my lawyer." This could be a red flag indicating you're being scammed.

Invent to Commercialize (a.k.a. Build a Business from Scratch)

These are the inventors who dream of being the ones to make the invention come alive. The invent-to-commercialize path is about transforming your invention into a thriving business, making it accessible to the world, and reaping the rewards.

This approach means not only creating a groundbreaking invention but also launching it into the marketplace, driving sales, and scaling up for success. You'll navigate through the complexities of production, marketing, and distribution, guided by your vision and the determination to see your innovation thrive.

The invent-to-commercialize path is about taking your invention out of the laboratory or workshop and putting it directly into the hands of eager customers. For many inventors, it's the ultimate step to transform your ingenious creation into a market-dominating success story.

Ideal Personalities

Empowered Visionaries: Entrepreneurs who embark on the journey to commercialize their invention themselves are driven by an unwavering vision for their creation. They possess a passion that extends beyond immediate gains, focusing on long-term growth and the satisfaction of building a business from the ground up.

Fearless Risk-Takers: Launching a business is not for the faint of heart. It requires a daring spirit that can weather the uncertainties and challenges that come with the territory. Entrepreneurs who choose to commercialize their inventions embrace these risks with open arms, ready to tackle whatever hurdles come their way.

Unyielding Resilience: Building a business is a journey marked by obstacles and setbacks. Those who take the reins of their invention are resilient, resourceful problem solvers. They have the tenacity to overcome roadblocks, adapt to changing circumstances, and persist in the face of adversity.

Their unwavering commitment drives them to push boundaries and redefine success.

Leadership: Entrepreneurs who find fulfillment in guiding teams, overseeing operations, and embracing the responsibility for their company's triumph often gravitate toward the self-commercialization model. These are the leaders who recognize that their zone of genius is creating the best possible start-up squad made up of people who bring all the talents and skills needed to launch and run a business effectively.

Experienced Business Pros: This path is ideal for those who have been in business before, are well-connected in their industry, and have their sales funnels working well. They have done this before, and they will do this again.

If your aim is simply to make money, then the invent-to-commercialize route is not for you because you would need to focus on building that start-up and guiding it to success. It is hard work, and if you aren't prepared to put the effort into the build, some of the end goals are not for you. But that's fine because, in later chapters, we will discuss what does suit you.

Scam-Watch (a.k.a. the Boxing Ring Insider Knowledge)

No matter what path you take, you are going to come across people who are only looking out for themselves; this path is overrun with them. In the innovation industry, they are a dime a dozen and can smell gullible people from a mile away.

These players, "inventor helpers," make a living off of hopeful inventors who need high-value contacts and want the promise of risk-free success. In this case, your best protection is a good lawyer and the willingness to put in the time and resources required to commercialize your invention in the most strategic way possible [*see more on inventor helpers in chapter 6*].

The invent-to-commercialize pathway is subject to far too many scams to list. My best advice is to stay vigilant. Here's how:

- Find a good lawyer, a good patent agent, and a good accountant. You need them, even though you may not know it yet.
- Put everything in writing. Agreements are essential. Many con artists have learned what to put in writing and what not to put in writing.
- Make sure agreements are fair to both parties. Con artists will try to convince you to sign

agreements with wording that only favors them. This is why you need to put the contract through your own lawyer (still not me). They are on your side and will fight for your rights.

- Use the right contracts for the right things. Too many times people try to rely on contracts meant for another relationship. A contract needs to accurately reflect your relationship and the rules of play of that relationship. It should not be a cookie-cutter contract. Each relationship is different and clauses need to be appropriate for that particular relationship.

- Monitor internal business activities. I work in fraud and data theft matters, and the amount of blind faith businesses put into staff still surprises me. Just because people are employees does not mean they aren't trying to con you—even employers will try it.

The Greater-Good Path (Get Rich v Save the World v Do Both?)

Dear P.I.T.C.H.ers, there is an unstated path that you *can* follow that doesn't lead to Money Town. Instead, it leads to Good Karma Town for the greater good.

Not all inventions are profit-driven. In fact, some

of history's most prolific inventions weren't. Instead of building a lifetime of financial riches for their inventors, these inventions were created to change the world for the better at a time when they were needed most. They were borne of inventors—who were scientists and engineers—fueled by a commitment to the greater good. By any moral measure, they were rich. But if you saw their bank balances, you may not have thought so.

CASE STUDY: Consider the case of Dr. Jonas Salk. Dr. Salk invented the polio vaccine at a time when the crippling disease took countless lives, permanently disabling roughly 35,000 people in the United States—and paralyzing half a million worldwide—each year, and leaving many with either brain or lung symptoms, paralysis, or years lived in an iron lung (an artificial respirator which used negative pressure to help patients exhale because their lungs no longer had the strength to do so). Many who survived ended up with leg braces, crutches, or a life in a wheelchair. Bottom line—at the time that Dr. Salk made his discovery, there was no cure and an urgent, worldwide need for a vaccine.

When Dr. Salk discovered the vaccine, he could have patented it for riches and reward, but instead, he refused to keep his discovery for himself. He was vocal in his belief that the vaccine's benefits should be accessible to all humanity. His decision to gift this life-changing invention has saved countless lives and remains an enduring testament to the power of selflessness in the realm of innovation. Dr. Salk's selflessness was paid not in financial riches, but in the knowledge that countless lives were saved as a result of his hard work and big ideas. ■

Now let's also consider the invention of the seat belt.

CASE STUDY: The three-vpoint seat belt, invented by Nils Bohlin, is another invention deserving of all the good karma it earned from saving countless lives. Bohlin came to Volvo as a safety engineer after years at SAAB working on ejection seats for airplanes. The reason that these seat belts are found in every car on the market today is because Volvo recognized the life-saving potential of the seat belt, and opted out of keeping it to themselves. They opened up the patent for the greater good.

Many inventors made changing the course of history for the better a higher priority than getting rich off one invention. Progress paired with compassion and dedication to humanity is the ultimate legacy for any inventor or P.I.T.C.H.er—one that will inspire generations to come. ▪

Choose Your Own Inventor Path

In short, each inventor must choose their own adventure—their own inventor path. If the Money Town route is your chosen path, IP protection armor is essential. Whether you want to lead, or, instead, dream of simply inventing and selling, there is a path that leads to getting rich from your P.I.T.C.H. just for you.

Your job is to play to your strengths and work with (or hire) those whose strengths are your weaknesses. That is the key to inventor success and money-making with your ideas. If you try to do it all yourself, without the right start-up squad and the right armor (IP protection), you're destined to lose in the boxing ring, at the jousting match, and any chance of taking up residence in Money Town.

CHAPTER SIX

BATTER UP—TIME TO PITCH

(a.k.a. Harness Your Capital)

Welcome to the dragon's lair, where savvy inventors (a.k.a. entrepreneurs with brilliant ideas <u>and</u> the right protection) become knights. Only the victorious will emerge unscathed. All else will fall prey to death by dragon fire … or con artists (the effects of which are eerily similar and equally painful).

In this dragon's lair, I delve into the meticulous art of crafting and delivering the perfect pitch to raise capital or sell assets. In the majority of cases, this is where you either make it or break it.

Pitch-crafting is more than just storytelling; it's a strategic performance. Understanding what investors seek, recognizing the stages of investment, and targeting the ideal backer for your current developmental phase and exit plan is essential.

Your pitch is your inventor's anthem. I'll help you make it resonate and inspire. I'll help you gain insights into investor psychology and pitch structure. Together, we will walk through real-world examples of successes and pitfalls. This chapter arms you with the tools not just to present but to captivate, persuade, and secure your idea's future, all under the power and armor of IP protection along the way.

Using the P.I.T.C.H. Method

This is where you learn how to pitch like a pro. It has all led to this, dear P.I.T.C.H.er! If you've read this book from cover to cover, you'll have completed P.I.T.C. and the H is your step toward making millions from your idea—with sage wisdom and a healthy dose of luck, of course!

Without harnessing capital for your invention through the right *sales P.I.T.C.H.*, your ideas will remain nothing more than that—ideas.

The P.I.T.C.H. Method is based on my twenty-five years of experience in:

- information technology, patents, trademarks, and other IP goodies,
- working with investors purchasing over $1 billion worth of IP assets,
- working with investors looking to secure investments,
- countless rounds fought in the boxing ring,

- the studying of thousands of invention success and failure stories by inventors across the globe.

Let's recap the P.I.T.C.H. Method before we dig deeper.

Prepare to Validate:

You must test the waters of reality and determine if your idea is a sinker or a swimmer. This is your litmus test of determining if the market is ready for your genius.

IP IQ:

Learn how, where, and when to protect your ideas from those who want to claim your ideas as their own.

Test Your Type:

Personality type plays a big part in the success or failure of an idea making it to market. Are you cut out to be a sole founder, or do you need a start-up squad? Discover the personality traits of successful start-ups and your strengths and weaknesses.

Chart Your Exit:

Now that you know your personality type and traits, learn the different end goals for inventors and decide what path to wealth you wish to take. Hint: you don't need to launch a start-up to make money from ideas. You could cash in as early as tomorrow.

Harness Your Capital:

Learn about investors, what they are looking for, investment and funding cycles, and how to pitch based on your stage of commercialization to achieve your chosen end goal.

Upon completion of this chapter, you'll have all of the knowledge you need to P.I.T.C.H. to investors and make your end goal a reality.

In the last chapter, you learned about your options for your invention's end goal or exit strategy:

1. **Invent to Sell**
2. **Invent to License**
3. **Invent to Commercialize**

No matter which path to profit you choose for your idea, at some stage, you are going to need to pitch. With a good idea and a well-crafted pitch, your opportunities are limitless.

Capital investment is eventually what you'll be looking (and pitching) for. In this chapter, we dive right into:

- The different stages of investment rounds;
- How to find an investor who is a perfect match for you and your product;
- What investors are craving;
- Where to find investors;
- How to break the ice with an investor;
- What your pitch should contain; and
- What to watch out for.

Investment Rounds Broken Down (a.k.a. When Do I Need Funding & For What?)

It's essential to understand the different stages of investment rounds if you're to have a good chance of navigating this path effectively. It will also help make sure you are pitching to the right investors.

A vast majority of you probably think you don't need to pitch because you are inventing to sell or inventing to license, but the process is the same. In all cases, you will likely need to obtain funds for your start-up. The contents of the pitch may change, but you still need to pitch.

Investment rounds are like chapters in your invention story, each with its own set of expectations, challenges, and opportunities. In the start-up world, there are stages through which external funding is raised, each serving a different purpose and type of investor.

But with great investment comes great responsibility. The more they invest the more they will want control. They will want to step in when things get bumpy to protect their investment.

In the ever-evolving journey of start-up funding, each phase—from pre-seed, to seed, to Series A, B, C, and beyond—has its own expectations and challenges. Understanding the nuances of each stage is crucial for success.

Pre-Seed Funding

Think of the pre-seed phase as laying the groundwork for success. This is when you bring your community of people together to share your idea and plans. Your goal is to get their buy-in.

For almost every inventor I know, the first round of funding they receive is from those closest to them, the people who want to share their success with you when you "hit it big." Parents, siblings, best friends, neighbors ... if you can see them sitting around the pool sipping mai tais with you, you may have your first set of investors.

The types of investors who invest at this phase are typically family and friends. Professional investors won't invest in this round because the idea is not proven and the risk is too high.

Seed Funding Rounds: Having a Booth at a Market

Seed funding rounds are all about building the market for your start-up and transforming your idea into a resilient contender in the business arena.

Seed rounds are about establishing the foundations, akin to setting up a vendor booth at a market. You're crafting your products, understanding your potential buyers, and getting ready to enter the marketplace on a bigger level.

Just as a vendor at a market invests in quality goods, branding, and an attractive setup, start-ups use seed funding to refine their IP, develop prototypes, and lay the groundwork for the journey ahead.

Series A: Opening Shop in the Town Square

This phase of funding is typically for optimizing products and gaining a loyal customer base. It's like moving from a small market stall to a prominent shop in the bustling town square, attracting venture capitalists to support this expansion.

You've proven your goods have local appeal. Now, with Series A funding, you will be able to expand your offerings, attract more customers, and solidify your presence.

Series B: Expanding to Nearby Towns

It's time to focus on expanding market reach and scaling. It's as if your successful shop in the town square has become a brand and now you're looking to open branches in nearby towns. Series B is focused on raising funds to establish those branches. Venture capitalists and private equity firms act as investors supporting this regional expansion. You are expanding but are expanding locally.

Series C: Going Global

You've reached the stage for scaling the company to new heights, including into international markets. It's like transforming your successful chain of local shops into a global franchise. Series C funding helps you take your marketplace concept to international markets. Investors, including venture capitalists, private equity, hedge funds, and investment banks will be interested now, joining you to support your ambitious expansion.

Series D and Beyond: Hosting Your Own Grand Marketplace

This is the pinnacle of the funding journey. Funding from Series D and beyond helps your thriving marketplace evolve into a grand city center, potentially leading to a public offering and attracting a diverse range of participants, including a variety of investors valuing the company for its proven success and future potential.

Decoding Tranche-Based Funding

In the labyrinth of venture capital and private equity funding, a common method of disbursing investments is in tranches based on achieved milestones. This is especially true for start-ups and growth-stage companies.

The tranche-based funding model operates on a delicate balance of progress and financial support. It is meticulously designed to mitigate the investor's risk while ensuring the company moves forward and succeeds as envisioned.

Unlike the conventional lump-sum approach, the total investment amount is fragmented into smaller, incremental payments known as tranches. Each tranche is judiciously released only upon the successful accomplishment of predetermined milestones, marking a departure from the highly sought-after issuance of unrestricted checks preferred by inventors.

These critical milestones are intricately defined during the negotiation phase and are often intricately linked to the company's performance metrics. Some of these metrics might include:

- pivotal stages in product development;
- revenue targets (such as the attainment of patent grants);
- customer acquisition figures; and
- other significant operational or strategic objectives.

As an illustrative example, a tech start-up might receive its initial tranche of investment upon completing the development of a prototype. Subsequent tranches could hinge on milestones such as securing a specified user base or reaching a predetermined revenue threshold. Further tranches might correlate with the achievement of growth metrics, market expansion, or the introduction of new product features.

This staged funding methodology stands as a guardian for the invention and the investor, ensuring tangible progress and steering the company toward success before additional capital commitments are made.

For investors, it acts as a risk-mitigation tool, offering checkpoints at each stage to assess the company's performance and potential before extending further financial commitments.

Simultaneously, for companies, it establishes a crystal-clear set of objectives and benchmarks, serving as a guiding compass that often accelerates and sharpens growth initiatives. It also puts the pressure on by demanding achieve-at-all-costs operational management from companies, knowing that any hiccup or setback could hold subsequent tranches hostage, which at that point, would be a critical lifeline for ongoing operations and sustained growth.

50(+) Shades of Green

Once you know what investors are looking for and the stage of investment you seek, it's important to understand that not all investors are created equal. Some will want the most profits in the least amount of time, some are willing to lower their profit goals for less risk, some will want all the market share, and others want to cut costs. It's essential to find the right investor who aligns with your vision and objectives and to make sure that whatever P.I.T.C.H. you deliver, it's the one that speaks to their particular shade of green.

The Dating Game

Let's look at finding the perfect investor the way you might look at finding your soulmate. You need to align with someone who shares your interests, your life stage, and most importantly, sees your worth.

The four crucial elements for your investor match are:

1. **Industry Alignment:** Seek investors who understand and have an interest in your industry. Opposites rarely attract when it comes to investors.
2. **Financial Capability:** Look for backers with the financial capacity to invest right now. Not all investors have money at any one time, and they tend to be a bit skint between investments. Trying to sell to investors who have no money right now is futile. Consider them off-limits until they're ready for a relationship.
3. **Development Stage:** Match your venture's maturity level to the investors who invest at that stage. Some investors like start-ups to be fresh so they can be mentored and guided. Some like them more mature. Most investors will only invest at

particular points in the maturity cycle of a company. This is one of the biggest complaints we hear from inventors: "Why aren't they interested, Nic?" It's not you, it's not them, it's the situation. The inventor's company maturity does not align with an investor's risk profile.

4. **Belief in You:** Your investors must believe in your vision and be willing to work with you to make it a reality. You would hope for the same from anyone you were building a future with. If you are to run the company, your investor will be assessing you to determine if you have the goods to make it work. If you don't, why would they waste their time or money getting involved?

If your potential investor thinks there's a chance you can make it work, they may opt to go ahead but with prenuptial-style protections (outlined below) in place to ensure performance.

Sometimes an investor will want to place a CEO in charge or have a person on the ground watching you. At the very least they will want a seat on the board table.

Only when all these elements converge do you have the perfect match. The last thing you want is to be in the middle of the P.I.T.C.H. and realize that your match is just a casual observer, doesn't have any cash flow, or doesn't believe in you. If they're not a match, swipe left and move on.

Understand Investors

I have acted for hundreds of investors over the years, and one thing investors all crave is the ability to get a return, which can be either monetary or some other intangible form. You would think this is blindingly obvious, but I have lost track of how many inventors become so focused on the invention that they lose sight of the fact the investor wants something out of the relationship.

Your Pitch Deck needs to spell out what the investor is to expect from the investment. Don't assume all investors want money. Some seek other things, such as changing a marketplace or giving back to the community.

In my world, the investor often obtains what they want through exclusivity. They want that competitive edge in the marketplace. Patents and other IP rights (a.k.a. your IP armor) offer this exclusivity, but it comes in various forms. Investors are keen on start-ups that can dominate their respective industries, with or without patented technologies. It may come in the form of a new paradigm-shifting idea; which is something so radical you need to educate consumers on what it is and why they should give up their normal way of thinking (think a teleporter from Star Trek). Or, it may come as an existing market share or exclusivity of a product.

But let's look at why that is. Simply put, exclusivity gives their investment in the company an advantage in trade. Advantages convert to more traction in the marketplace and, ultimately, a far more successful (and profitable) business.

Savvy investors may see a company being run badly with high overheads and low profits, but they know how to cut down on overheads and increase profits without needing to bring in more income. The savvy investor knows an opportunity when they see it.

Another reason investors buy a company is to gain access to assets.

Imagine there's a company called ACME Co that writes software for a particular industry and has eyes for another company in a completely different industry. ACME Co knows the other company's software will complement their own, and they want in. So ACME Co does what any self-respecting IP-rich company does: they buy that other company, take a copy of the source code, and sell the company as a going concern whilst notifying the new buyer that ACME Co reserves its rights to the software in its own industry. The new buyer doesn't care because they aren't in the same industry as ACME Co. This brings taxation benefits but also gives them free access to the software.

Software sells for big bucks, imagine buying a company for $100 million and then selling it three months later for $110 million but keeping a copy of the source code—you just got $100 million worth of source code for free, and you pocketed $10 million for your troubles.

Don't assume that if your company is not profitable investors won't want in. They often see value where others don't.

There are also some techniques used by companies that are so effective, they are illegal in some countries. If ACME Co is doing really well, and I mean *really* well, it rules the marketplace. As it does, it watches out for competition that might be a threat to its market share. It spots a start-up that is doing well but needs some funds, so it buys that start-up and then it shuts it down. Suddenly the competition is gone.

Another technique is to use your buying power to make life difficult and costly for your competitors. Let's say ACME Co has a conveyor belt in the factory and some bright spark has launched a start-up to revolutionize the conveyor belt industry. The invention is so good, it speeds up production by 80 percent. Amazing.

Obviously, your competitor wants this invention as well. Who doesn't want to make more money? So you do what any self-respecting IP-rich company does: You buy that bright spark's company, including its invention, and you either run the company and keep the revolutionary invention to yourself or you take the IP for yourself, robbing your competitor of the opportunity to use the money-saving technology. Again, sometimes this is so effective it's illegal. Watch yourself.

Risky Business v Safe Bet (a.k.a. Metrics that Matter to Investors)

With so much at stake, investors are not likely to write checks without thoroughly weighing their chances of success. This process of evaluation is called due diligence.

Professional investors scrutinize potential investments with a keen eye. They know what to look for from experience, evaluating various metrics and criteria to identify promising opportunities and bad bets. Understanding what investors look for is key to crafting a pitch they can't resist.

Market Potential: Investors seek start-ups with the potential for substantial market growth. They want to know that there's a significant demand for your product or service. A large addressable market indicates more room for expansion and higher returns on investment.

Team Strength: Your start-up squad is a critical component of the evaluation. Investors look for founders and key team members with the right blend of expertise, experience, and commitment. They want to see a team capable of executing the business plan and overcoming challenges with the right mix of personality types. Think of *Shark Tank*-style shows. When the investors are asking about the inventor's background and their team, they are evaluating team strength. Translation: Can we trust your team with our money?

Traction: Traction refers to your start-up's progress and achievements. Investors assess whether your product or service has gained real-world validation. Metrics like user adoption, revenue growth, and customer testimonials demonstrate traction and prove that you can execute your business strategy. Investors will prefer to invest in particular points in the growth cycle of a company. Some will not invest unless the idea is proven with some market traction. This frustrates inventors because they need the funds to get the traction—it's a *chicken v egg* thing.

Scalability: Scalability is a fundamental consideration. Investors are interested in businesses that can grow rapidly without proportionally increasing costs. Scalable start-ups can capture more market share and generate substantial returns for investors.

Business Model: Investors analyze your business model to understand how your start-up generates revenue. They look for monetization strategies that are sustainable and aligned with market trends. Are you going to launch your start-up in a crowded marketplace with well-established players? Or are you looking for investment to get your IP filed worldwide so you can sell to those big players with your IP in place? Without IP, you would be starting up knowing the big players will copy you as soon as you hit the market. Your business would be suffocated. That's a bad bet.

Competitive Advantage: Having a unique selling proposition or a competitive advantage is a significant attraction for investors. They want to know what sets your start-up apart from existing or potential competitors. This is where IP rights and unique ideas can help.

Intellectual Property and Barriers to Entry: Investors often favor start-ups with intellectual property protection, such as patents or trademarks.

Their IP protection creates barriers for others to enter the market, giving them a competitive edge.

Exit Strategy: Investors are interested in your long-term vision and exit strategy. Whether it's going public (IPO*), or acquisition or to sell onto the competition, having a clear plan for how investors will eventually realize their returns is crucial. *When a private company first offers its stock for sale to the public, it's called an Initial Public Offering (IPO). Essentially, an IPO marks the change from private to public ownership for the company.

Founder's Equity Stake: Investors may consider the founder's equity stake in the company. A significant founder's stake often suggests confidence in the start-up's potential and alignment of interests with investors.

Social Impact and Sustainability: Some investors prioritize start-ups with a social impact or sustainability focus. They look for businesses that not only generate profits but also contribute positively to society and the environment. Giving back is good branding.

Industry Trends and Market Timing: The timing of your start-up within a specific industry or market trend can be a critical factor. Investors consider whether your start-up is positioned to ride the wave of an emerging trend or address a pressing problem.

Wrapping Up Risk Assessment

Investors conduct thorough due diligence to assess the risks associated with your start-up. This includes legal, financial, and operational assessments to ensure transparency and mitigate potential pitfalls. Again, don't expect them to write you a check after the first meeting. They will want to clear the way for the investment and set down the ground rules, which takes time.

Never underestimate the criteria by which you or your pitch is being judged. By addressing these aspects in your pitch presentation, you'll demonstrate to investors that you've considered their perspective and that your start-up aligns with their investment goals and expectations.

Sourcing Your Investors (a.k.a. There's No App for That... Oh Wait...)

So, you know how you want to make money from your idea, and you know what investors are looking for, you know your metrics, but you don't know where all the investors are, particularly ones with pockets deep enough to buy, license, or commercialize your invention.

Unless you've done this a dozen times before, finding investors for your start-up can be challenging. But if you don't figure it out, you'll never secure the funding needed to bring your business idea to life.

Your first step in finding an investor is to go where the investors are! Don't expect them to come to you. It's up to you to seek them out. You just need to bite the bullet and make the first approach.

Remember—the money you're looking for in funding rounds isn't to "fund" yourself and your bank account, a common misconception. Rather, it's funding to support your invention into becoming something more, something bigger, something worth buying and selling in whatever exit strategy you choose. When you remind yourself of this, you'll find it much easier to source and P.I.T.C.H. your opportunity to investors.

It's interesting to note that some startups fall into a Ponzi-scheme-like trap, which can lead to their downfall. Picture this scenario: An investor puts money into a startup during a funding round, aiming for a quick exit in the subsequent round. This investment gives the startup what's known as "runway"—industry jargon for the amount of time the company can cover its ongoing expenses before it runs out of cash. The idea is that the company must "take off" before this runway ends.

However, this is where things can start resembling

a Ponzi scheme. An investor puts in money but plans to exit at the next funding round. Consequently, the responsibility for the company's future falls onto new investors. This cycle can continue, with each new investor hoping to exit in the next round, until it becomes clear that the startup isn't achieving the necessary growth or success. At this point, finding new investors becomes challenging. Prospective investors see that the company isn't taking off as expected and become hesitant to invest, leading to a situation where the startup struggles to secure further funding and faces potential collapse.

* * *

Here's a list of where to find potential investors:

Family and Friends: Don't overlook the possibility of seeking investments from your personal network. Family and friends who believe in your idea may be willing to contribute. Your family and friends will often invest earlier in your maturity cycle, mostly due to their financial ability.

Angel Investors: These are individuals who provide capital in exchange for equity or ownership stakes in start-ups. You can find them through personal networks, entrepreneur clubs, and online platforms dedicated to connecting start-ups with angel investors. Angel investors often invest smaller amounts in twenty or more companies hoping that one will pay out. They use a "machine gun" approach rather than a sniper approach. Angel investors will often not invest in later stages of development. They want to get in and get out quickly.

Venture Capital (VC) Firms: These are professional investment organizations that manage pooled funds from multiple investors. Research VC firms that specialize in your industry or start-up stage and pitch your business to them directly. Venture capitalists will want a proven idea, they will want to see a working prototype, and they'll expect you to have some traction in the marketplace.

Crowdfunding: Platforms like Kickstarter, Indiegogo, and GoFundMe allow you to present your project to the public and request small contributions from many individuals. This method can be effective for raising funds and creating a buzz around your start-up. Watch out for this method because in some lands you will need to pay taxation on the money received if you trade investment for stocks or products.

Business Incubators and Accelerators: Many cities and regions have business incubators and accelerators designed to help start-ups grow. These organizations often provide funding, mentorship, and resources to selected start-ups. This puts you together with like-minded individuals and, importantly, broadens your networks.

Networking: Speaking of networks, attend industry-specific events, conferences, and meetups to expand your network and connect with potential investors. Engaging in local entrepreneurial communities can lead to valuable introductions.

Pitch Competitions: Many organizations and universities host pitch competitions where start-ups can win cash prizes or attract the attention of investors. Participating in these events can be an excellent way to showcase your business and hone your pitch. Always ask for feedback after a session, and don't get offended when you get it—it isn't always what you want to hear.

Online Platforms: Online platforms like AngelList, Crunch-base, and Gust facilitate connections between start-ups and investors. You can create profiles for your start-up and explore potential investment opportunities. Websites like *Rightes.com* allow you to advertise your IP for sale, license, or even find an investor. It's currently free to advertise on *Rightes.com*. Use it to your advantage while you can!

Corporate Investors: Some established companies have venture arms or investment divisions. If your start-up aligns with a corporation's interests or goals, they might be open to investing.

Institutional Investors: Institutions like banks, insurance companies, and pension funds occasionally invest in start-ups. Although these are typically larger deals, they can provide substantial funding.

Online Presence: Maintain an online presence through a professional website, LinkedIn profile, and social media. This can attract inbound interest from investors who discover your start-up online organically or even via paid ads.

Legal and Financial Advisors: Consult with professionals, such as patent lawyers, patent agents, accountants, and financial advisors. They may have connections in the investment community and can introduce you to potential investors. Many patent agents also have a collection of investors who want to invest in your industry. Lean on them and they may help you pave your path with gold.

Remember that finding the right investor isn't just about securing funds but also about finding a partner who believes in your vision and can provide valuable expertise. Networking, clear communication, and persistence are key when seeking investors for your start-up.

Sourcing Your Buyers/Licensees

If you are going the invent-to-sell or invent-to-license money-spinner route, you are going to be pitching to a different kind of audience. This audience is predominantly going to be whomever your competition would have been if you had gone into business. Remember the competitor analysis you did in Chapter 1? It will become invaluable here.

Think of the chain of how products get to market. There is a manufacturer who creates the product, the wholesalers who then sell them directly to retailers or to others in the middle of the supply chain. The wholesalers (which may include large brands) push products into retail stores and other retail outlets. Then there are the retail outlets themselves who sell to the end buyers.

Manufacturers normally manufacture to order. This does not rule them out as a target, though, because there are thousands of manufacturers who would love to add to the products they supply. Some manufacturers also throw in freebies for customers to see if there is any interest in the product. If they find that there is, they go into production.

As to the middle suppliers, there are two types—those who buy wholesale to sell at the retail level and those that do the same thing, but only produce their own goods. The latter ones are the ones you want to target.

Some suppliers don't own IP themselves, they prefer to license it from others and pay a royalty to be able to sell those products. It is the ultimate hat tip to inventors.

As to the retailers, you can approach the stores to see if they are interested, but it is not common to see retailers themselves interested in buying the IP for a product. Where your opportunity lies with retailers is approaching them with a novel way of doing business or suggesting they break into a different market and planning out how that would happen, all under the protection of your IP armor, of course.

But Nic, How Do I Even Get a Foot in the Door? (a.k.a. Landing Meetings with Investors)

So you've identified your stage of development and the types of investors you will target and where to meet them. *But what's next, and how do I get an appointment with these mythical creatures?*

Once you find potential investors, you need to weed out the ones that are not suitable with a direct opening question.

Here is a good example of a one-question pitch:

"I have invented a chemical that stops tires going flat, and that doesn't degrade over time. I see that you invest in the automotive industry. We have functional prototypes and lab research showing the efficiency of our product. It has a potential marketplace of 500 million sales per year. We are seeking an investment of $x million to allow us to firm up our pending IP rights around the world and take the product to market. Are you looking to invest right now and are you interested in meeting to learn more?"

This pitch is crafted well:

- Starts strong with an opening that grabs
- Immediately identifies a problem statement
- Identifies the solution
- Explains the benefits of our solution
- Spotlights the market potential
- Ends with a call to action.

It's a simple approach, but with one question, you have worked out if the investor has money right now, if they are prepared to invest at your company's maturity stage, and whether they are interested in the industry.

You don't need to follow any specific order as long as the primary components of the pitch are present, covering all the bases your potential investor will want to hear. If nothing else, I recommend at least starting strong and ending with a call to action. You will find your groove the more times you pitch. Go with whatever gets you that next meeting, as long as it's not misleading. Any claims you make in your pitch will need to be backed up with proof.

This is a good example of an invent-to-sell or invent-to-license pitch:

"I have invented a new kids toy designed to be a cheap impulse buy that keeps kids entertained. Patents are in place. It has a potential marketplace of fifty million sales per year. We are looking to offload the whole patent family. Are you interested in meeting to learn more?"

Again, it is a simple but smart approach. It may work well because:

- Describes the solution
- Even though the problem is not directly stated, every parent will understand the problem
- Describes our end game, which is to sell
- Makes it clear there is something to sell – our patents

- Ends with a call to action.

No Means No

Now, dear P.I.T.C.H.ers, no means no. Seriously. So if they say no, don't hound them. Hounding doesn't work; it just makes you annoying, and it's the fastest way to make an investor run for the hills! When you hound them, all the investor thinks is, "This person is a nightmare. If they are like this now, what will they be like later? <groan> I do not want to deal with this person. I need to run away."

Once they respond with a "thanks but no thanks," politely write back to thank them for their time and ask if they know of anyone who might be interested in investing. Ask if they're willing to either give up the name or provide an introduction. Not all strangers will introduce you to their networks because they see an introduction as an endorsement—they don't know you from a bar of soap so don't be offended; it isn't personal, it's business.

Quick Tips: What do you need in place to start talking to others?

1. Obviously, start with an idea or invention;

2. Get asset protection advice and put it in place before you file registrations for your IP;

3. Ideally, you will file your IP protections first so as to have them in place before you talk to investors, potential team members, or any others;

4. Get an NDA in place which has a provision that you (as the inventor) own the IP in the technology even if the other side contributes to the invention. Use those NDAs when speaking with all others (some professionals have an obligation of confidentiality so the NDA may not be needed for those people);

5. Ensure those you are using to help you develop the IP have assigned the IP to you, through written contracts (some countries don't require this);

6. Continue to use your NDA after you have filed your protections as you may "tinker" with the invention and you want those improvements to be protected as well. This will protect you when/if the other side suggests changes and you want to own those as well.

How to Pitch & Get Rich (Hopefully)

Your "pitch" is your sales pitch. Whether you think you do or don't need one—you will. While some pitches are formal and others informal (we'll get into that in a moment), the pitch is where you ask others to believe in your invention and put money behind it.

A formal pitch contains the following elements:

- Clear identification of a problem that exists in the marketplace,
- Overview of the marketplace (including customer types and size),
- Explanation of how the invention solves the problem in the marketplace,
- Mention of protections that are in place to give the investor exclusivity, and;
- Who you are and what you want.

This sounds a lot like the opening I mentioned above. That is because the opening is a pitch in itself. You want to give a short-form (elevator-style) pitch, such as a thirty-second or two-minute pitch just to help you get your foot in the door. Once in the door, you can get into more detail and share your full, detailed pitch via your pitch deck.

Your pitch is a data-driven analysis of the worthiness of your ideas and if you were paying attention in the idea validation chapter, you, dear P.I.T.C.H.er already have the answers!

Your pitch's success hinges on piquing the interest of your audience.

When you present to potential investors, the aim is not to secure an immediate investment. It's to leave them eager to delve deeper into your concept. A successful pitch is the start of a relationship that should progress to the negotiation and investigation phase.

What is Your "Why"?

People buy not just what you do but *why* you do it. Include your purpose—identify the problem to be solved (the problem scope)—and identify why you are solving the problem. Then, follow with how you solve it and then provide a brief explaining more on the solution (your invention). Remember to include the outcome for people who buy your solution—e.g., in our car charger example, allowing electric car drivers to travel distances with the confidence that they will be able to charge their cars on the go.

Step 1: Build Your Pitch

Pitch decks need tailoring for different investment rounds. Most inventors go "all-in," swamping the investor with unnecessary details in rounds that are only meant to entice.

Keep it concise. A pitch is not a brain dump. Overwhelming your audience with information may do more harm than good. I've witnessed P.I.T.C.H.ers who were so overwhelmed and excited that they talked their investors *out* of investing. Better to button it. Answer what they ask, give them what they need and want, and then let them decide if taking a risk on you and your idea is an investment they are willing to make. Your role here is not to teach potential investors how much you know or how smart you are. Rather give them a teaser to entice them into other discussions.

Step 2: Tailor Your Pitch

One size does not fit all when it comes to pitch presentations. You will want to tailor your pitch for different audiences and maturity levels. Use the following to see what key elements you need to include in your pitch deck for specific investors at different investment rounds:

Investment Stage: Pre-Seed

Key Elements:

1. Vision and mission
2. Problem and solution
3. Market opportunity
4. Basic business model

5. Start-up Squad introduction
6. The Ask/Call To Action (CTA)

Investment Stage: Seed

Key Elements:

1. Enhanced business model and value proposition
2. Market analysis and target demographic
3. Traction and early customer feedback
4. Product or service demo
5. Financial projections
6. The Ask/CTA

Investment Stage: Series A

Key Elements:

1. Detailed market analysis
2. Proven business model and revenue
3. User growth, engagement metrics, and traction
4. Strategic plan for scaling
5. Current financials and future projections
6. The Ask/CTA

Investment Stage: Series B

Key Elements:

1. Market positioning and competitive analysis
2. Detailed customer and user analytics
3. Scalability plans and expansion strategies
4. Financials and future projections
5. Team expansions and management structure
6. The Ask/CTA

Investment Stage: Series C

Key Elements:

1. Market dominance and leadership
2. International expansion plans
3. Advanced financial metrics and profit-ability analysis
4. Long-term strategic vision for growth and innovation
5. Exit strategy or plans for further rounds of funding
6. The Ask/CTA

Step 3: Determine Your Ask

At some stage you need to state what your idea is

worth, what you want, and what you are prepared to give up. Unfortunately, this is where those with inventor syndrome raise their heads.

We have all seen it on the *Shark Tank*-style shows. A hopeful entrepreneur walks in and makes what they hope is the perfect pitch. Their eyes light up as they describe how amazing their invention is and how the investors need to buy it now—like *right* now!

Then the investors ask their questions and reality sets in.

INVESTOR: Is there a prototype?

INVENTOR: Um, yes, of course, sure ... I'm working on that ...

INVESTOR: Are their sales?

INVENTOR: No ...

INVESTOR: Have you filed your IP protection?

INVENTOR: Yes.

INVESTOR: Great! [Now we are getting somewhere]

INVENTOR: But they aren't granted yet.

INVESTOR: Have you done any trials to be sure it works?

INVENTOR: Well ... No ... But it will work! Trust me!

INVESTOR: And what are you looking for in an investment?

INVENTOR: $20 million for 10 percent of the company.

INVESTOR: Um yeah. We're out.

Inventors have to be realistic. If you have an untested product, no minimum viable product, and no sales, why on earth would any investor invest a fortune in your company?

The answer is simple: They probably won't.

Typically pre-seed investments are funded by family and friends and they generally only raise about $10,000-$20,000 in that funding round. This investment is also known as "love money." Alas, here we are, watching an inventor asking for $20 million on national television for an invention that hasn't yet been proven to work. An idea would have to be very special indeed for those to invest that amount at that level!

Let's do the math. At $20 million for 10 percent, this bright-eyed, bushy-tailed inventor is valuing their company at $200 million ($20 million x 10). Just think about that for a moment. They are asking someone to sink $20 million into a company that has no guaranteed IP rights, no prototype, no sales, and no proof it even works. It's no surprise that a pitch like this would receive unanimous nos. Even the hungriest carnivorous fish-style investor is going to pass up this potential meal. They can taste the regret an ocean away.

Remember, the investment ask is also relevant to properly realized and foreseeable potential. An investor may well pay $20 million for an early buy into a teleportation company. But they will pay that for a "beam me up Scotty" experience, not a "scatter my atoms through time and space" experience.

Dear P.I.T.C.H.ers, if you're to have a real chance of raising funds and landing the right investors, it's crucial to be realistic about what you are asking. As an inventor and entrepreneur, it's your job to walk into the pitch with a purpose (other than overnight riches) and to be clear about your *ask*. Too many inventors don't know what they want out of it. Being desperate for a deal—any deal—is not a purpose but it is all your potential investors will see. If you appear willing to take any deal offered, you aren't helping the investor narrow down how they can help. You have to know what you want, before you ask for help.

Step 4: Build and Nurture Investor Relationships

Building strong investor relationships is essential for the long-term success of your venture. Learn the art and science of networking, transparency, and trust-building to create fruitful collaborations.

Investing in someone's idea is investing in them.

It's essential to have trust and transparency from the patent owner/inventor to the investor. Remember to send regular updates to investors to keep them apprised (and excited!) about their investment.

You'll also want to continue to network both inside and outside of your industry. Building partnerships, alliances, and affiliations that can bolster your venture's success.

Investors may also want to place a person on the ground. Expect them to demand a seat at the director's table—this is the investor's right hand, their insider tasked with keeping them abreast of developments with the company, giving them an opportunity to voice their concerns and suggestions.

There is always a sign I look for in companies to determine company health. That is whether the investor's director still has a place at the round table of the board room. Many countries have directors' duties. That means that a director has certain fiduciary duties to protect the company and one of those duties is to not trade when insolvent. Breaches of directors duties are a very serious thing and directors can be barred from being a director if they breach their duties.

An investor wants to protect its right hand. So if a company appears to be faltering and you find that the investor has pulled its director from the board room without replacing them, be very cautious about why. What happens in the boardroom stays in the boardroom and you might not have the full story.

You can also expect that the investor may want someone in the office to keep an eye on the operational activity of the company.

Watch out for the people who try to manipulate and who know what to put in writing and what not to put in writing. This is a separate personality type all of itself. The "do as I say but I won't put my name to it" type of business person is someone to look out for. They say one thing in person but another in writing. They are slippery little suckers, hard to pin down. After meetings, summarize the meeting and send emails detailing what was decided. Make sure you honestly summarize meetings and decisions and have a written record. Send the email to the other person because that is that person's opportunity to object and say that other things were decided.

If you receive one of those emails, ensure it is accurate and not misleading. Because when you show that email in court, the other side will twist what they said to mean something else entirely. It's all relevant in the boxing ring.

Step 5: Delivery

Your job is to walk into the pitch cool, calm, and collected (think Buddhist monk on morphine), and say: "We have a winning and novel invention, our legal protections are in place, the marketplace is $XX billion, the time in the marketplace is now, the idea is proven in the marketplace, and we are ready for action."

If you have a proven track record, you can add: "We've successfully launched products like this before, we know the market, and we say this will be a successful launch. Buy in now, or the opportunity will go to someone else."

When presenting your pitch, the KISS Method is key (keep it simple, stupid). And also, keep it relevant. While you may be an expert on the subject, the pitch is not the place to showcase your intelligence.

Do not draw in connections that are not logical—it only makes you look unprofessional, desperate, and, quite frankly, unhinged.

Don't name-drop. It makes you look desperate. And you never know who knows who. Word might get back to that person that you are trying to get a deal off their back.

I watched a pitch once about gardening without herbicides, suddenly they brought in discussion about a named famous person and how he would love the idea. Not relevant and that person had no idea about the invention. The connection was too tenuous, the audience was lost, and the inventor looked desperate. All the potential investors simply looked at each other and shook their heads. People said, "He had me until the [insert name] part." He lost the room and the investment.

Avoid overloading your pitch with irrelevant information that may have potential investors running for the hills. This isn't a general chat at the football game or campfire. It's a pitch. Keep it focused and compelling for your audience.

Scams by the Inventor against the Investor (a.k.a. the Boxing Ring for the Narcissist or Conflicted)

"Why can't they cut me a check, Nic? Why are they asking me all these questions?"

The answer is simple. The investor wants to get what they're paying for by making sure they're investing in something real. Perhaps they've been stung before, or have heard some of the boxing ring stories. Looking deeper into your proof, claims, promises, and paperwork is due diligence, an act of protection against being scammed. It's not personal, it's business.

After all, investors can be just as much a victim of scams as inventors can be. These scams involving investors and IP-rich companies can take various forms, often revolving around misrepresenting the intellectual property's value, potential, or ownership.

Let's look at a few examples of common scams:

The Overvalued Patent Scam: In this scam, a tech start-up claims to have developed groundbreaking software with a patented algorithm that promises to revolutionize the industry. Eager to invest in cutting-edge technology, an investor conducts minimal due diligence, swayed by the patent's supposed exclusivity and potential. After investing a significant sum, it's discovered that the patent is either non-existent, cannot be patented, or is vastly overvalued, with no real potential for commercial success. The investor is left with a worthless stake in a company whose main asset was hype.

The Stolen IP Scam: Here, a biotech company claims to have exclusive rights to a revolutionary medical process. An investor, enticed by the potential for high returns in the lucrative field of medical technology, buys into the company. Later, it was revealed that the IP was actually stolen from another researcher or institution, leading to legal battles (entitlement disputes) and the investor's funds being tied up in a company now facing lawsuits and a tarnished reputation.

The Phantom Tech Scam: You know this one. A start-up presents an innovative medical technology that tests for thousands of conditions based on one drop of blood. The company claims its technology, backed by proprietary data, will disrupt the market. Investors dazzled by the demonstrations and fearing missing out on the next big tech breakthrough, invest heavily, and continue to invest heavily.

It later turns out that the technology was vaporware, all smoke and mirrors—it didn't function, the lab results were fabricated, and the technology was far from being market-ready. Investors are left with a substantial loss as the company folds under the weight of its false claims. It's fraud and it's the real-life story of Theranos.

The Misrepresented License Scam: In this scenario, a renewable energy company claims to have an exclusive global license for a revolutionary solar panel technology. An eco-conscious investor, excited by the potential impact and profitability, invests a large sum.

After some time, it is revealed that the license was either non-exclusive or restricted to a much smaller geographical area. The investor finds themselves part of a far less lucrative venture, with limited market potential.

The Pyramid Scheme Disguised as IP Investment: A software company claims to have developed a unique platform and encourages investment not just in the company but in spreading the word to other potential investors. The initial investor recruits others, receiving bonuses for each new investment.

As it turns out, the company's actual product is minimal or non-existent. The primary business model is the pyramid scheme itself. Once recruitment slows down, the scheme collapses, leaving investors with significant losses.

Scams by the Investor against the Inventor (a.k.a. the Bait and Switch)

Scenarios where an inventor is scammed by an investor also present a range of deceitful practices. Here are some sucker-punches that inventors need to watch for.

The Equity Grab Scam: An eager inventor with a novel green energy device meets an investor who shows great interest in the invention. The investor offers to fund the project but insists on a majority equity stake, citing risks and the need for substantial capital.

The inventor, desperate for funding, agrees. Over time, the investor dilutes the inventor's share through additional funding rounds and contractual loopholes, eventually leaving the inventor with a negligible stake in their own invention. Worse, the investor may control the board room (or shareholders) and may assign the IP rights away from the company leaving the inventor high and dry, holding nothing more than an empty company.

The IP Theft Scam: An inventor with a prototype for an advanced medical instrument is approached by a seemingly reputable investor. During the negotiation process, the investor requests detailed technical information, purportedly to assess the project's feasibility. After receiving the information, the investor breaks off communication and uses the provided technical data to file for their own patents, effectively stealing the invention. The lesson here is to verify everyone. It is all too easy to fake an identity these days.

The Predatory Loan Scam: An inventor needing quick funds to patent and develop a new software tool is offered a loan by an investor under extremely high interest rates and unfavorable terms, disguised as a helpful gesture.

As the inventor struggles to meet the steep repayment terms, the investor leverages the debt to take control of the invention and the underlying company, leaving the inventor in debt without their creation.

The Fake Accelerator Scam: An inventor is invited to join an exclusive start-up accelerator program, promised access to top-tier mentors, investors, and a host of resources.

The program requires a significant upfront fee. Once paid, the inventor finds the program to be a facade—minimal mentorship, no real investor connections, and subpar resources.

The investor running the program disappears with the funds, and the inventor is left with a lighter wallet and a project that is no further ahead than when they started.

The Market Monopoly Scam: An inventor with a groundbreaking agricultural tool partners with an investor who promises to handle the business aspects, including market introduction.

The investor deliberately restricts the product's market entry, creating artificial scarcity while secretly developing a competing product.

Once the competing product is ready, the investor floods the market, undercutting the inventor's tool and effectively monopolizing the market with their version.

The "Inventor Helpers" Scam: This is a scam I see repeatedly. In this scam, someone offers to introduce you to a world of contacts that can help make your invention dreams come true. They say they can lead you to the people who will invest in you and your company, but in reality, they're taking you for a ride.

These coaches and consultants present themselves as "inventor helpers." They typically take the form of the person who *claims* to have previously had success, has great connections, and can introduce you to a gazillion potential investors who are eager to invest in your venture, license it, or buy you out. They promise just about everything an inventor could hope for... all for a price. They appear to be helpers, but in large part, they're anything but!

Dear P.I.T.C.H.ers, here's where it gets sticky. Some of these people are legitimate and *do* have those connections. But many don't. Many inventor helpers aren't about finding people to exploit the invention because they are too busy exploiting you!

Normally, they will "help" you for a period of time, say six months or a year. You will pay them a monthly fee, and in return, they will introduce your invention to their connections. If a deal is made, they will get a cut of that deal. It could be any percentage. I've seen people want up to 80 percent of what you earn from the deal.

On top of any potential royalty-sharing, you'll be asked to "commit to the experience" by paying a monthly fee. If you try to cut down the commitment time, they will argue that finding investors takes time (which is true), and then accuse you of not committing to the process. Their goal is to get you to jump in with both feet. At the end of their sales tactics, you find yourself manipulated into the deal without even knowing how it happened. They may or may not be able to deliver on contacts and investors, but they are often very good at selling their fairy-tale services.

Once your investor helper tries and fails to land investors or deals, they'll begin blaming the invention, the marketplace, the timing—or better yet, *you*—for their failure.

When you come close to the end of their six or twelve-month contract with no deals or investors to show for it, it's common to be told they *have a fish on the hook* and are close to a deal, or the *marketplace has moved and now is the time* because *they can just feel it*.

So how do you distinguish which of the two they are? The catch is, without a deal, it is next to impossible to determine if they are actually trying to market your invention or if they're just living off the monthly fee you're paying them. If you do get wise and walk away, they will likely move on to another victim.

These people often play their cards close to their chest. You have no way to know if they have reached out to an investor on your behalf. If you ask for any proof, you'll be told there isn't any because their investor network is "confidential." Another reason for this is they don't want you doing a deal with the investor on the side and cutting them from the deal.

So, how do you know they are even trying to find investors or just using you for that monthly fee? You don't. Some will be stringing you along and taking you for a ride.

So, how do you know if they are worth your time and money? Make them prove themselves. They say they have experience—that's great, maybe they do—but can they prove it? Here's where they often go quiet. You ask them about their experience and they say they can't tell you because of confidentiality agreements they've signed. Frustrating. Particularly because it's sometimes true.

Regardless, even if this inventor helper is legitimate, it's up to you to find out if their experience is even relevant to you and your invention. Is it relevant to helping start-ups? *After all, it's really easy to be successful in an already-established successful company.* It takes a different skill set to find deals for start-ups. They should be able to show you how they introduced a new product or thing into the marketplace, preferably *your* marketplace. They have to show a good track record of successfully delivering to others the very service they are offering to provide for you.

Ask for evidence that your invention is being pitched to others. Ask to join the pitch and be involved in the process. At least then you know the person is doing what they are paid to do and negotiate (hard) the amount of money, or cut, this person is set to receive.

All of the scams above underscore the vulnerabilities inventors can face when dealing with investors *and* the red flags to watch out for. Inventors should always conduct thorough background checks on potential investors, conduct thorough due diligence, and seek qualified legal counsel when negotiating terms to protect their interests and intellectual property.

CHAPTER SEVEN

CHANGE THE WORLD

Dear P.I.T.C.H.ers, in this book, we've embarked on a journey through the intricate landscape of turning your big ideas into goldmines. But as we reach the final chapter, I challenge you to reach for inspiration and dare to dream of changing the world. Because as inventors, you are the ones who can.

You are standing at the crossroads of invention and destiny. The path you choose from here can be a catalyst for transformation, not only in your life but in the world around you. You possess the tools, the knowledge, and the unwavering spirit to embark on a journey that transcends mere financial gain. It's a journey that carries the promise of creating a lasting impact on humanity.

My best advice to you is to embrace **the power of purpose**. Remember that the greatest inventions in history didn't just fill a market gap or generate profits, they solved real-world problems and enriched lives.

To change the world, begin by asking yourself:

"What problem do I want to solve? Whose lives can I improve?" Your invention should resonate with a deep sense of purpose. It should be a beacon of hope, a solution to a challenge, or an enhancement to the human experience.

Remember that **protecting your ideas** isn't just about locking them up; it's about building the foundation on which your business can thrive. Intellectual property isn't just a shield, it's ammunition that amps up your competitiveness, blasts open doors to new markets, and, when you play your cards right, can be a money-making machine.

Whether you picked up this book and skimmed it for the bits that piqued your interest, or devoured it cover-to-cover, turning your creative inventions into wealth is no small matter. The back-and-forth negotiations and battles of **the boxing ring** are very real, which is why it can be daunting (and so essential) to learn about what to expect in the ring. You need to know how to protect yourself every step of the way.

Look at **idea validation** as the golden bridge between your big dreams and the real world. It's not just a confirmation, it's a magical process that sculpts your idea into a solution that will truly connect with your audience. This bridge isn't just a pathway; it's a direct route to the heart of your audience (a.k.a. those people willing to pay for your big idea) where loyalty turns into sales.

I contemplated writing this conclusion as song lyrics, a rhapsody, or even a valedictorian speech for you, dear P.I.T.C.H.ers, but in truth, it doesn't need to be. You already know your invention is worth something. Now use the tools inside this book to make sure the rest of the world knows it too.

While ideas are sexy, protection is sexier. Here's the advice I wish every single inventor was given before they risked it all for their dreams:

- Never underestimate the value of **shareholder agreements**. More than just paperwork, they're the peacemakers that ensure every voice at the table is valued and decision-making is smooth.
- In the world of connections, it's not just about what you know; it's about who you know. **Networking** isn't just a list of contacts; it's a lively ecosystem around your business. It's where opportunities pop up, mentorships take root, and challenges become stepping stones. Your network is your go-to for inspiration, resources, and support.
- As you embark on your invention adventure, it is often best to avoid the murky waters of co-ownership. Instead, embrace the spirit of

co-invention. Pick your **start-up squad** like you're assembling *The Avengers*—selectively.

- Beware of being afflicted with **inventor syndrome**; it's like a fog that can cloud your judgment. Stay sharp, and let your ideas soar—with the right crew.

- Celebrate challenges and embrace failures along the way. When you **love the losses as much as the gains**, you build resilience, adaptability, and a flexible spirit. Challenges aren't roadblocks, they're invitations for growth. Each lesson is a step toward a more badass and innovative business model. The path to changing the world is rarely without obstacles. Edison faced over a thousand failed attempts before creating a practical light bulb that could be made accessible to the general population.

- Learn from the past but **don't dwell on the past**. Steve Jobs[17] left his own company in 1985 and did not return to it until about ten years later, at which point he led Apple to new heights. These setbacks weren't failures; they were stepping stones toward monumental achievements. Every obstacle you encounter is an opportunity to learn, adapt, and grow.

17   Wikipedia contributors. "Steve Jobs." Wikipedia, February 19, 2024. https://en.wikipedia.org/wiki/Steve_Jobs.

Remember, it's not the absence of obstacles that defines success, but the perseverance in overcoming them.

- **Protecting your wisdom with IP is your secret weapon**. Make decisions today that fortify your future. Your legacy is born from these decisions. Remember this: Your **ideas are the seeds of change and innovation**. Nurture them, protect them, and watch as they transform not just your future but the future of those around you. You are the world-changers, the idea-creators, the big-thinkers, and the ones whose impact is guaranteed ... as long as you protect it.

In truth, I started, just as you are—a creator, inventor, engineer, and ideologist. My ideas were the catalyst to becoming an Intellectual Property lawyer, a career centered around helping people like you and me protect that which we create.

Changing the world with your invention isn't confined to the boundaries of your product or service. It's about creating a ripple effect that extends far beyond your initial idea. It's about inspiring others to dream, innovate, and contribute to a brighter future. As architects of innovation, we are also catalysts of change. Your success can become a catalyst for positive change in your community, your industry, and even the world at large.

Your ideas can and will change the world. And as such, you deserve to be seen, heard, and rightfully compensated on your epic journey. It has been my delight and pleasure to guide you through the gauntlet of invention. It's been a rocky ride at times. But if you take away nothing else from this book, please take this: for the love of invention, protect and profit from your ideas by hiring your very own lawyer and patent agent. Visit *GetRichFromThePitch.com* for a referral to a patent agent. My curated list of agents is constantly updated with only the best of the very best.

As we conclude this journey through the world of commercializing inventions, I leave you with this thought: The power to change the world resides within you. Your ideas, your passion, and your unwavering commitment to creating a solution have the potential to leave an indelible mark on history.

Your journey doesn't end with a patent or a product launch; it *begins* there, fueled by purpose, guided by innovation, and defined by the legacy you choose to create. Let your inventions not only make you prosperous but also leave the world better than you found it. In the pages of history, your story awaits, inspiring generations yet to come. The world is ready for your invention.

So, dear P.I.T.C.H.er, are you ready to step boldly onto this path and follow the light from that spark that has ignited within you? Are you ready to start a ripple effect?

Now it's time for you to go forth and P.I.T.C.H. your ideas!

Nic

The End

…just kidding.

Your journey doesn't end here. This is just the beginning for you. I hope that as you've read through this book, you've also been filling those notebooks with ideas and innovations worth developing and pitching.

Join the P.I.T.C.H. Squad

Share Your Ideas: Visit us at *GetRichFromThePitch. com* to let us celebrate your achievements! Your journey could inspire a fellow P.I.T.C.H.er and create a ripple effect of innovation.

Show Us Your P.I.T.C.H. Moments: Caught in the act of reading? We love seeing P.I.T.C.H.ers in action! Share your photos, reading the book. Tag us on social media @getrichfromthepitch, use the hashtag #getrichfromthepitch and let the world see your dedication and enthusiasm.

Stay Informed: Sign up for our newsletter at *GetRichFromThePitch.com* to get the latest updates straight to your inbox. Be the first to know about exciting developments, new resources, courses and opportunities that can propel you further on your path to success.

Find the Right Support: Looking for a patent attorney

or agent? I've got you covered. *GetRichFromThePitch.com* is a treasure trove of referrals and contacts to help you protect and propel your brilliant ideas.

Time to Steal the Show? Got ideas that could rock the world? Sign up at *GetRichFromThePitch.com* for our thrilling pitch competitions for a chance to showcase your innovation to the world – it's more fun than being a mere spectator (unless you're just here for the popcorn).

Learn and Grow: Keep an eye out for our upcoming masterclass courses designed to sharpen your skills, expand your knowledge and fill your brain. As a P.I.T.C.H.er, you're always growing, and I'm here to support that growth every step of the way. Join the waitlist for my upcoming masterclass courses that guide you through the P.I.T.C.H. Method and teach you so much more at *GetRichFromThePitch.com*. My masterclasses take GET RICH from the P.I.T.C.H. to another level. Be quick, spaces are limited.

Follow Nic:

LinkedIn: *https://www.linkedin.com/in/nicolemurdoch/*
Instagram, Facebook: @getrichfromthepitch

Your story is important, your ideas are valuable, and

your success is our success. At *GetRichFromThePitch. com* you will find other entrepreneurs and inventors like yourself, inventor resources, and more. Let's keep the conversation going, the ideas flowing, and the victories coming. Remember, every success story starts with a single P.I.T.C.H.! Let's hear yours.

GLOSSARY

In the realm of investor pitching and the world of innovation, an understanding of legal concepts and intellectual property rights is paramount. While this is, by no means, an exhaustive list, here are a few of the terms you'll want to become familiar with:

Angel Investor: An affluent individual who provides capital for a business start-up, usually in exchange for convertible debt or ownership equity.

Assignment: The transfer of rights or property from one party to another, often used in the context of transferring intellectual property rights, such as patents or copyrights.

Benchmark: A standard or point of reference against which things may be compared or assessed.

Bootstrapping: A self-funding approach where an entrepreneur starts a company with personal finances or the operating revenues of the new company.

Boxing Ring: A colloquial, metaphorical term for litigation, particularly in the context of intellectual property disputes. It implies a combative, aggressive approach to legal challenges.

Commercialization: The process of bringing a product or invention to market, often involving marketing, distribution, and sales. Investors are interested in the commercialization plans for the innovations they support.

Confidentiality: In a business or professional context refers to the principle or practice of maintaining the privacy of information shared between parties. It involves an agreement or a duty to not disclose or share proprietary information, trade secrets, or any other sensitive data to unauthorized parties or the public. Not to be confused with copyright.

Copyright: A form of protection for original Works of authorship, such as books, music, and software. When discussing content in your pitch, understanding copyright rules and fair use is crucial. Not to be confused with confidentiality.

Crowdfunding: The practice of funding a project or venture by raising small amounts of money from a large number of people, typically via the Internet.

Caution P.I.T.C.H.ers, these may be illegal where you live or have taxation implications.

Design: In the context of intellectual property, a type of intellectual property protection that gives the holder exclusive rights over the visual design of an object. This protection is usually given to the appearance or aesthetics of a product, and it can include aspects such as shape, configuration, pattern, ornamentation.

Dilution: Dilution occurs when additional equity or ownership shares are issued, which can reduce the percentage ownership of existing shareholders, including investors.

Due Diligence: An investigation or audit of a potential investment or product to confirm all facts, such as reviewing financial records, plus anything else deemed material. Due diligence involves the comprehensive investigation of a start-up's legal, financial, and operational aspects. Investors conduct due diligence to evaluate the risks and potential of an investment.

Equity: In the context of investor pitching, equity refers to ownership shares in the start-up. Investors typically receive equity in exchange for their investment.

Exclusive License: Grants one party the exclusive

right to use, make, sell, or license a patented invention. It can be a valuable asset when seeking investment or partnering with others.

Exit Strategy: Outlines the plans for how investors will eventually realize returns on their investment, such as through an acquisition, IPO, or other exit event.

Incubator: An organization designed to accelerate the growth and success of entrepreneurial companies through an array of business support resources and services.

Infringement: The violation of an intellectual property right, such as unauthorized use of a patented invention.

Intellectual Property (IP): Intellectual property refers to creations of the mind, such as inventions, literary, and artistic Works; and symbols, names, and images used in commerce. IP rights include patents, trademarks, and copyrights, among others.

Invent-to-Commercialize: This pathway involves developing a product or technology not just for the purpose of invention but with a clear plan for commercial exploitation. It means the inventor or the company is focused on the entire process from the initial idea and invention stage to bringing the product to the market. This can include activities like market research, product development, securing funding, manufacturing, and sales strategy. Essentially, it's a holistic approach that encompasses both creating the invention and successfully launching it in the market.

Invent-to-License: In this approach, the inventor develops a new product or technology and then licenses the rights to use, manufacture, and sell it to another party. Instead of producing and selling the product themselves, the inventor profits from the invention by receiving licensing fees or royalties from the licensee. This strategy is often used when the inventor prefers not to handle the commercial aspects of the product or lacks the resources to manufacture and market it.

Invent-to-Sell: This exit strategy involves creating an invention with the goal of selling the intellectual property rights in the invention.

Investment: The action or process of allocating capital or resources with the expectation of generating an income or profit. In the context of the innovation industry, this often means putting money into start-ups, business ventures, or funds with the expectation that these entities will grow and generate financial returns.

Investor: An individual, company, or financial

entity that allocates capital with the expectation of receiving financial returns. Investors typically assess the potential growth and profitability of ventures or assets before committing their resources. In the innovation industry, investors might include angel investors, venture capitalists, or entities like investment funds that specifically focus on start-ups or emerging technologies.

Joint Venture: A business arrangement in which two or more parties agree to pool their resources for the purpose of accomplishing a specific task.

Key Performance Indicator (KPI): A set of quantifiable measures that a company uses to gauge its performance over time.

Lawyer/Solicitor: A professional who practices law, providing advice and representation in legal matters, a.k.a. someone who writes a 10-page piece of advice and calls it a *brief.* Careful dear P.I.T.C.H.ers, not all lawyers specialize in intellectual property or patent law.

License: A permission granted by the patent holder to another party, allowing the use or commercialization of the patented invention.

Litigation: The process of taking legal action

or resolving disputes in the court system, a.k.a. the boxing ring.

Monopoly: In the realm of patents, a monopoly refers to the exclusive rights granted to an inventor or their assignee by the government. This legal monopoly allows the patent holder to exclude others from making, using, selling, or importing the patented invention for a limited period, usually twenty years from the filing date of the patent application.

Motsa: Australian slang for a large sum of money, a fortune, or a great amount, especially as won in gambling.

Non-Disclosure Agreement (NDA): A legally binding contract that aims to protect sensitive information shared between parties, such as during an investor pitch. It establishes confidentiality and sets forth the consequences of disclosing confidential information without consent.

Open Slather: Australian or New Zealand slang for no restrictions or a free-for-all.

Own Goal: British slang for a goal scored against your own team. Also an act that you think will help yourself but ultimately harms you.

Patent: A legal protection granted by a government that gives an inventor exclusive rights to their invention for a specified period, typically twenty years. In the context of pitching, presenting a patented invention can enhance its attractiveness to investors.

Patent Agent: A professional authorized to represent inventors before the patent office and assist in the patent application process. They typically have a technical degree and have passed exams to qualify as a patent agent. Unlike patent attorneys, they typically do not have a law degree. In some countries, patent agents are referred to as patent attorneys.

Patent Attorney: A qualified legal professional who specializes in intellectual property law, particularly in obtaining and protecting patents. Often used interchangeably with patent agent or patent lawyer, depending on the country. They may or may not be able to represent clients in patent offices, may or may not be a lawyer, and may or may not have passed a specific patent exam.

Patent Lawyer: A lawyer specializing in patent law, including patent application, enforcement, and litigation.

Pre-Seed Funding: This is often the earliest

funding stage for start-ups, where funds are used to support the initial development and formation of the business. Pre-seed funding is typically used for market research, product development, and building a management team. This stage of funding usually involves small amounts and may come from the founders, friends, family, and angel investors.

Prior Art: Refers to all publicly available information and related inventions that existed before a specific invention. Investors may investigate prior art to assess the novelty of your invention.

Problem Scope: Refers to the clear definition and boundaries of the problem that an invention or innovation aims to address. It involves understanding the specifics of what is to be solved or improved.

Prototype: An early sample, model, or release of a product built to test a concept or process. It is a term used in a variety of contexts, including semantics, design, electronics, and software programming.

Runway: In the context of investments, particularly when talking about start-ups and new business ventures, refers to the amount of time a company can continue to operate before it runs out of money.

Seed Funding: The first official equity funding

stage. It typically represents the first official money that a business venture or enterprise raises. Seed funding helps a company finance its first steps, including things like market research and product development. With seed funding, a company will usually be expected to be turning a profit or be ready for the next round of funding.

Series A Funding: The first significant round of business financing by venture capital funds or investors for a company offering equity in return. Series A funding is typically used to optimize product or service offerings and market fit, as well as scale the company.

Series B Funding: This funding round is about taking businesses to the next level, past the development stage. Investors help start-ups get there by expanding market reach. Companies that have gone through the seed and Series A phases have already developed substantial user bases and have proven to investors that they are prepared for success on a larger scale.

Series C Funding: Companies that make it to Series C funding sessions are already quite successful. These companies use Series C funding to help them develop new products, expand into new markets, or even to acquire other companies. Series C funding is focused on scaling the company, growing as quickly and as successfully as possible.

Series D Funding: This round of funding is somewhat less common than the earlier rounds. Companies that go for Series D funding might do so because they are seeking one final round of funding before going public, or because they need a little more help to achieve the level of success they've been working toward.

Shareholder Agreement: A legal document that outlines the rights, responsibilities, and obligations of shareholders in a company. It is an important tool for preventing conflicts within a company by clearly defining the roles and expectations of all parties involved. It's particularly critical in privately held companies where shareholder issues can directly impact the day-to-day operations and future of the business. Key elements of a shareholder agreement include ownership structure, voting rights and decision making, dividend policy, management and operation of the company, transfer of shares, dispute resolution and exit strategy.

Trade Mark: Trademark is spelled as two words in some countries, which is why you will see both spellings occasionally used in this book.

Trademark: A symbol, word, or phrase (or something) used to identify and distinguish goods or services of one party from another. Registering a trademark can protect a start-up's brand identity and value.

Unicorn: A term in the venture capital industry to describe a privately held start-up company with a value of over $1 billion.

Venture Capital: A form of private equity and a type of financing that investors provide to start-up companies and small businesses that are believed to have long-term growth potential.

Work: Under the *Copyright Act*, a "Work" refers to the expression of ideas, and not the ideas themselves. This can include literary, dramatic, musical, and artistic Works such as poetry, novels, movies, songs, computer software, and architecture. The copyright does not protect facts, ideas, systems, or methods of operation, although it may protect the way these things are expressed.

RESOURCES*

Canadian Intellectual Property Office (CIPO):
The federal agency responsible for intellectual property in Canada. https://www.ic.gc.ca/eic/site/cipointer-net-internetopic.nsf/eng/home

Creative Commons: Provides a set of flexible copyright licenses and tools that enable sharing and reuse of creativity and knowledge. https://creativecommons.org/

EAGLEGATE: For all your Australian legal needs. https://eaglegate.com.au

Espacenet: Provided by the European Patent Office, offering access to over 120 million patent documents. https://worldwide.espacenet.com

European Patent Office: Provides access to searching European patents, information on patent law and policy, and guidance on the application process. https://www.epo.org

European Union Intellectual Property Office (EUIPO): Manages the EU trade mark and the registered community design. https://euipo.europa.eu

GetRichFromThePitch.com: Your go-to resource for all things innovation and success. Share your success stories, show us your P.I.T.C.H. moments, find the right support, join pitch competitions, learn and grow and more. https://getrichfromthepitch.com

Google Patents: A search engine for patents and patent applications from multiple patent offices. https://patents.google.com

Insurance: Visit *GetRichFromThePitch.com* for a referral to insurance agents.

Intellectual Property Office of New Zealand (IPONZ): The agency for granting and registering IP rights in New Zealand. https://www.iponz.govt.nz

Intellectual Property Office of the United Kingdom (UKIPO): The official UK government body for intellectual property rights. https://www.gov.uk/government/organisations/intellectual-property-office

IP Australia: The Australian Government agency for intellectual property rights. www.ipaustralia.gov.au

Mothers Of Invention: Women in Technology: This book celebrates women in technology, and the people who inspired them. https://amzn.asia/d/1ISqvil

Office for Harmonization in the Internal Market (OHIM) - European Union: Responsible for managing the EU trade mark and the registered Community design, OHIM offers registration of trademarks and designs that are valid in all EU member states. https://www.euipo.europa.eu/en

Patent Agent/Attorney/Lawyer: A great resource to find a patent agent, patent attorney or patent lawyer. Visit https://getrichfromthepitch.com and follow the links.

Patent Scope: A tool provided by WIPO for searching international patent applications and accessing related documents and information. https://patentscope.wipo.int

Queensland Tourism: Discover Queensland, Australia's vibrant blend of stunning natural wonders, from the Great Barrier Reef to the Daintree Rainforest, paired with thrilling adventures and tranquil tropical islands, all under the warmth of endless sunshine. https://www.queensland.com/au/en/home

Rightes.com: A website for IP owners to advertise IP rights, for sale, license or investment and for IP buyers/investors to buy, license or invest. https://Rightes.com

United States Copyright Office: Provides important resources for copyright registration and information in the United States. https://www.copyright.gov/

United States Patent and Trademark Office (USPTO): The U.S. federal agency for patents and trademarks. https://www.uspto.gov

WIPO Academy: Offers distance learning and face-to-face courses on various aspects of intellectual property, suitable for different levels from beginners to experts. https://www.wipo.int/academy/en/

WIPO - Global Brands Database: Managed by the World Intellectual Property Organization for information on global trademarks - caution, not all countries are displayed. www.wipo.int/branddb/en/

World Intellectual Property Organization (WIPO): A global resource for IP services and education, WIPO offers extensive information, including databases for international IP research and tools for IP protection worldwide. https://www.wipo.int

ACKNOWLEDGMENTS

To the brilliant minds and tireless spirits of the inventors who have contributed to this journey, my deepest gratitude. It is your willingness to challenge the status quo, to fail and try again, that drives humanity forward. May this book honor your contributions and inspire future generations of inventors.

To the tinkerers, dreamers, and garage workshop warriors, your passion and creativity fuel the continuous evolution of our world, often without recognition or fanfare. Your ability to see beyond the conventional and transform the 'impossible' into reality is nothing short of extraordinary. Don't stop being you.

A colossal thank you to my book coach, Crystal Adair-Benning, and my editor, Jennifer Goulden. Together, they have achieved the impossible: not just coaxing a complete book out of me, but doing so with grace and humor. These two remarkable women deserve a medal, or at least a lifetime supply of coffee, for their patience, skill, and sheer willpower. I'm profoundly grateful for your perseverance, your talent, your raw honesty, and, most importantly, your belief in this project and in me.

To the readers, I hope my words help you. You've got this!

To my clients, without whom this book would have no purpose. Your need for an entrepreneur's survival guide has shaped every word. Your role in this endeavor is immeasurable and deeply appreciated.

A massive shoutout to my family, for their infinite patience with my quirks and chaos. You're the unsung heroes in this sitcom called life! Surprise plot twist – my children are indeed my own flesh and blood. Sorry kids, you can't escape the gene pool. You're stuck with me.

NICOLE "NIC" MURDOCH, BEng (Elec), JD (HONS 1), MIP, FIPTA, GAICD, is an Australian legal practitioner, Registered Trade Marks Attorney and Engineer, as well as the Founding Principal and Director of EAGLEGATE Lawyers in Queensland, Australia. Murdoch is trained as a Patent Agent, is a graduate of the Australian Institute of Company Directors (AICD) and is a fellow of the Institute of Patent and Trade Mark Attorneys of Australia (IPTA). She has spent her life innovating and creating things that didn't exist before—an inventor at heart and in her work. Her first degree was a Bachelor of Engineering, which laid the foundation for a decade-long career in the IT sector. Murdoch went on to obtain a Juris Doctor, a Master of Industrial Property, and open a law firm specializing in technology protection and litigation. At EAGLEGATE, she collaborates with innovators, inventors, entrepreneurs, and investors, guiding them as they transform ambitious ideas into market realities and taking legal action to defend their rights when they are violated. Her unique combination of engineering and legal expertise makes Murdoch an authority in her field. In writing *Get Rich from the P.I.T.C.H.*, Murdoch shares her own five-step framework for breaking down many of the barriers that entrepreneurs face in their pursuit of success. Murdoch lives in Brisbane with her husband Vern, two children, and two fur babies.

Made in United States
North Haven, CT
27 May 2024

53005956R00159